the soviet naval offensive

an examination of the strategic role of soviet naval forces in the east-west conflict

naval institute press
annapolis, maryland

edward wegener

the soviet naval offensive

translated from the german
by henning wegener

This book is an updated and expanded
translation of *Moskaus Offensive Zur See*.

Maps by Wolfgang Vater

Library of Congress Catalogue Card No. 74-31738
ISBN 0-87021-671-6

Printed in the United States of America

contents

preface to the american edition

The spectacular naval armament of the Soviet Union since World War II is an event of global political significance. Literature on the subject is predominantly descriptive and the emphasis is mostly on types of ships, weapons systems, and the quantitative balance of forces on both sides.

This study does not propose to engage in this kind of stocktaking. Rather it relates to Soviet strategic objectives at sea, their operational possibilities and limits, and the political effects that emanate from the overseas presence of Soviet naval forces in peacetime. The purpose of this study, then, is evaluation rather than description.

For assessment and evaluation, the book can of course not do without a certain number of technical facts. Without them, it would be impossible to appreciate the tactical capability of Soviet naval forces. But without tactical insights, one cannot dare make an assessment in the field of strategy. Of itself, the state of the art in weapons technology has no intrinsic value. It must be measured against the capability of the competitor. For this reason, the Western side—notably the U.S. Navy—must also enter the picture. In order to arrive at an overall judgment, one's viewpoint should be from the highest possible level. Only from there is the panorama complete, and are the dimensions right. In this sense, we intend to assess three overriding aspects of the Soviet offensive at sea.

First, we shall examine the conditions under which naval warfare appears possible in the nuclear age. We shall ask how the importance of sea power is to be evaluated in our time. A system of naval strategic concepts will be used to supply the yardstick by which Soviet armament and its potential effects in war can be measured. The conceptual framework relating to circumstances of war will then be supplemented by an analogous system for concepts relating to "maritime strategy" in peacetime. This process will enable us to assess the political effects of using fighting ships in peace.

With the aid of these conceptual systems, a clearer-than-usual distinction can be drawn between sea power in war—including the political effects that it generates in peace—and the effects of mere peacetime presence. This distinction is to be the second aspect of our analysis. It will also demonstrate the interdependence between the two sets of concepts. Haziness in the delineation between sea power and maritime power has all too often been the cause of faulty judgments.

The third aspect relates to geography. The difference in relative value of the naval strategic-geographical positions of the Soviet Union on the one side and the West on the other is not always recognized and followed through to its final consequences. In this respect, too, our set of naval strategic concepts provides a useful basis for assessment. It may be that a German author is particularly qualified to appreciate the geographical element. Germany, after all, has learned by painful experience in the course of two world wars what consequences may flow from a geographical position that is extremely disadvantageous in relation to the oceans.

Edward Wegener

Kiel, Germany

the soviet naval offensive

1

naval strategy in the atomic balance

Sea power and mastery of the sea

Naval warfare is concerned with shipping routes. This was true in the past, is true in our time, and will remain true in the future. He who can put these shipping routes to use for his own commercial and military transports, and manage to exclude the adversary from their use, brings about a condition that is referred to as *mastery of the sea*.[1]

Mastery of the sea may be global, or it may relate to specific areas. He who can acquire this mastery in war, in a particular sea area and over an extended period of time, can exploit the economic resources of countries that are accessible by sea, make them depend on him politically, and—if necessary—bring his military might to bear across the seas and onto their shores. If mastery of the sea is limited to the sea areas adjacent to one's own territories, the military purpose is frequently of primary interest: in defensive terms, to protect one's own territory; in offensive terms, to be able to invade territories of the enemy. He who does not possess mastery of the sea is, in wartime, confined

[1] It was an American admiral, Alfred T. Mahan, who first defined mastery of the sea as control over shipping, and who placed that concept in the center of strategic and historical naval considerations. The British naval historian Sir Julian Corbett based his thinking on Mahan's general ideas. *See* Edward Wegener, "Theory of Naval Strategy in the Nuclear Age." *U.S. Naval Institute Proceedings*, May 1972.

to his own continent, economically, militarily, and hence also politically. His power ceases at the very coasts of his territory.

To achieve or maintain mastery of the sea, one needs *sea power*. Naval forces alone do not constitute sea power. The mightiest fleet might as well be non-existent if it cannot reach the ocean where mastery is to be exercised and stay there for a period of time, ready to engage in combat. In other sea areas such a fleet might be useful or even vital. For the ocean area under controversy it is without significance (e.g., the Soviet fleet in the Caspian Sea). In order to constitute sea power, the fleet must have a *naval strategic-geographical position*.[2] By this is meant a coastal base or strip—possibly an island—situated *at the disputed sea area*, and equipped with at least one harbor that can serve as a base for gaining, exercising, or defending mastery of the sea. For this purpose, the position must possess all the facilities required to maintain the long-term fighting capability of the naval forces stationed there. It must be defensible against attacks from land, air, and sea. From the harbors of the base it must not only be possible to prevent the movement of enemy shipping, but to move one's own sea traffic, and indeed to keep it moving. This last function is particularly important.

To achieve all this, the naval strategic position must be linked with the source of power at home, either by land via efficient lines of communication, or by sea across an area under one's own mastery. Naval bases that are scattered all over the world and cut off from the home country by the enemy's mastery of the sea in between, do not constitute a naval strategic position, even though they may be well equipped and generously supplied. It is particularly advantageous to have at one's disposal a system of positions around the disputed ocean. This makes for operational flexibility, e.g., NATO positions around the Atlantic. Naval forces that have only one position available are, by contrast, at an operational disadvantage.

[2] We owe the concept of "geographical position" to Mahan. However, he evaluates relative advantages and disadvantages in the geographical situation of a given country and the configuration of its coastline, more in terms of operational possibilities. He makes no reference to naval strategy proper. In the naval wars that he describes, all the belligerents had a position on the disputed sea. The possibility that one side might have no direct access to the disputed sea area did not occur to him. But that lack was the determinant naval strategic fact for Germany in both world wars, as it is for the Soviet Union in our day. Accordingly, the concept, in deviation from Mahan, will here be referred to as *naval strategic-geographical position*.

The means of military power that make up sea power are referred to as a *fleet*. This term should not by any means be understood as referring to a firmly knit unit of battleships or aircraft carriers. Rather, it should refer to a force comprising all naval types, including, for example, submarines that can serve to fight the enemy's fleet with some prospect of eliminating it. A ship- and/or land-based naval air force is an indispensable component of a modern fleet.

Sea power thus consists of two elements, a "fleet" and a "position." It is a product of these two equally important factors, both of which are indispensable. If either of the two factors is zero, then the product is also zero. This is to say: Without a fleet, position is worthless and, vice versa, without position a fleet means nothing. Only the two combined make up sea power.

A third element is needed: a *sea-oriented mentality (seehaftes Denken)*[3] on the part of a people, especially of its leaders and its government. Clear recognition of the significance of the sea and of its domination is essential if the enormous efforts required to create and maintain sea power are to be made; only with such mental prerequisites can a politically and strategically efficient use of sea power be expected.

A sea-oriented mentality is indeed of the highest importance for the formation and the use of sea power. However, because of the significance of this vital element, it should be attributed to politics and overall strategy, rather than to sea power.

No matter how one categorizes a sea-oriented mentality, it is in fact the focus for the creation of sea power and for the inclusion of the sea in any political and strategic planning. Here the wisdom and perspicacity of the ruling personalities play as much of a role as do the historical experience and intellectual maturity of a nation. In this respect, national character, as history has shaped it, can have a decisive effect. Nations with maritime traditions of long standing are, in this respect, instinc-

[3]Many naval writers list more than three constituent elements of sea power. In Chapter I of *The Influence of Sea Power Upon History*, Mahan gives six. Two of them, "national character" and "character of the government," seem to comprise what we mean by sea-oriented mentality. Several of the elements Mahan listed pertained to the era of sailing ships and are now outmoded. The general tendency today is to limit the list to a very few elements of timeless validity. The present author believes that the three elements here mentioned—fleet, position, and sea-oriented mentality—are sufficient, and sufficiently comprehensive.

tively superior to nations whose military experience has been continental and territorial. Germany provides an example of a one-sidedly continental way of thinking. Neither the German people nor their successive rulers have ever managed to free themselves from the dominance of continental traditions. For this reason, Germany has never become a sea power—one of the major causes for her loss of two world wars.

To whatever extent a naval tradition may be helpful, it is not by any means an indispensable prerequisite for a sea-oriented mentality. The determination to build a fleet, to procure naval strategic positions, and to develop long-term naval strategic concepts is an intellectual achievement. It is especially likely to be based on purely rational grounds—as a consequence of lessons taught by history—in cases of deep concern over a nation's chances of survival, perhaps by an eminent statesman like Themistocles or by a ruling hierarchy like the Romans during the First Punic War. Similarly, only the realization that political or strategic objectives cannot be fulfilled without sea power can give rise to a sea-oriented mentality—and it can do so even in cases such as that of the Soviet Union, where every historical and natural precondition for sea power is missing. This, then, leads to the question: has Soviet Russia performed the transition from a continental to a sea-oriented mentality?

We will indeed have to discuss this question.

Naval strategic offensive and defensive

Mastery of the sea is the true aim of all naval warfare. Only if it is obtained can the double task of protecting one's own and preventing the enemy's shipping be fulfilled. For this reason, mastery of the sea supplies the standard against which a naval strategic concept must be measured. He who aims at mastery of the sea adopts an offensive naval strategy. He who possesses mastery will set about defending himself against such offensive; in terms of naval strategy, he is on the defensive. But one who renounces mastery of the sea altogether is obviously also on the defensive. This is so because, among other things, by renouncing mastery of the sea one exposes one's own coasts, and it becomes necessary to organize one's coastal defense against a potent naval enemy and to deploy substantial armed forces, either at sea or on land.

Whether the overall strategy of a naval war be characterized as strategically offensive or defensive is certainly not determined by the particularities of individual operations or by tactical behavior in combat. It is quite possible for offensive operations to be carried out in the framework of a strategic naval defense—for example, the German High Seas Fleet in the North Sea during the First World War—or for operationally defensive behavior to be adopted within an offensive strategic concept. What counts in characterizing a strategic naval concept is the ultimate objective with regard to mastery of the sea.

There are three possible ways in which a nation that initially has no way of exercising mastery of the sea can proceed:

Launch a strategic naval offensive, i.e., fight the adversary's mastery of the sea, and attempt to replace him. Such an offensive aims at reducing to zero one of the enemy's factors of sea power. This can be achieved either by eliminating his fleet or by seizing his position. If a fleet is present, but position is lacking, a strategic naval offensive starts with the creation of a naval strategic position at the disputed ocean, or, if there is a position but it is not satisfactory, by moving it forward geographically. Action of this kind does not fall to the navy alone. In peacetime it is a political task, and in wartime it is an objective of overall strategy. Thus, it is entirely possible for the army to make a decisive contribution to naval war by acquiring a position, or by taking one from the enemy.

Renounce a fight for mastery of the sea, i.e., adopt a defensive naval strategy. Such renunciation concedes to the enemy the fruits of mastery of the sea. A nation that lacks sea power is reduced to a defensive strategy, no matter whether that lack is due to the absence of a fleet comparable to the enemy's, to the absence of position, or to both.

Seize the object of naval war, i.e., the enemy's transport vessels, while deliberately renouncing mastery of the sea and avoiding combat with the enemy's naval forces. Taking or sinking the enemy's merchant ships is a recognized form of naval war. It is referred to as *raider warfare*.

Raider warfare

Historically, raider warfare derives from piracy and has much in common with modern partisan fighting on land.

Since aerial reconnaissance even over the ocean has become possible, the days of surface ships hiding for long periods in the "infinite oceans" have gone forever. Today, in a possible East-West conflict, raider warfare conducted by surface vessels would be unthinkable. Apart from aircraft surveillance, submarines have largely taken over the role of raiders. The submarine's ability to dive means that it can sojourn in sea areas where the enemy maintains mastery and circumvent his naval forces. The submarine has thus become the raider par excellence of our days. Inasmuch as the word *raider* refers to the surface raiders of former times, the term *raider warfare* has lost some of its meaning. However, it continues to be used as a professional term. Substitutes that writers have recently tried to introduce, have not found acceptance. They lack either precision or scope.[4] The traditional term *raider warfare–guerre de course* in French, *Kreuzerkrieg* in German–appears to be firmly entrenched in international usage.

Raider warfare might very well coincide with a contest for mastery of the sea. One can maintain, or fight for, mastery of the sea in one ocean area, and simultaneously conduct raider warfare in another. However, exclusive concentration upon raider warfare has, as naval history proves, never been successful in wresting the final victory from an enemy who had mastery of the sea. It was largely because of this fact that Mahan declared mastery of the sea to be the only worthwhile objective of naval warfare. Two successive German failures in submarine warfare seem to prove him right. But in our industrial age, which has made most countries dependent on sea communications, raider warfare, especially of the submarine variety, has gained a new dimension. Because of its immediate economic impact it can be almost as effective as sea power. If conducted against a nation that is dependent to an extreme degree on sea traffic, it could even

[4] The term *submarine warfare* is not, as may be thought, synonymous with *raider warfare*, since submarines can also be the instrument of a systematic fight against the enemy's fleet. Nor does the term *submarine blockade* convey the same notion. A blockade, as defined by international law, presupposes effectiveness, i.e., a high degree of enforcement, and that cannot be established by raider warfare with submarines. *Tonnage war* would be a suitable term for the kind of submarine warfare Germany carried on during both World Wars. Raider warfare by submarines is conceivable, not to maximize destruction of enemy vessels, but primarily to interdict systematically vital strategic transports, e.g., in order to prevent the reinforcement of a particular invasion area by sea.

produce *decisive* results. Yet, raider warfare remains, in principle, the weaker form of naval warfare. For not even the most successful raider warfare can open the important shipping routes to one's own shipping. We can conclude, therefore, that raider warfare signifies renunciation of mastery of the sea and is, in the last analysis, indicative of a naval strategic defensive.

Sea power in the nuclear age

The naval strategic concepts here described are based on the experience of the pre-nuclear period. To what extent can they claim validity under the different conditions that exist in the nuclear age?

Is not naval warfare that has mastery of the sea as its ultimate objective, obsolete? Some authors do in fact hold that view.[5] For them Mahan's and Corbett's naval strategy is dead.[6] To their minds, naval forces can now play a role only in a "limited war," in the framework of crisis management, or on other occasions short of war.

Admittedly, under today's conditions of nuclear balance a war between the two world powers is less probable than it was before. Still, it remains a distinct possibility. All the armament effort on land, in the air, and at sea, in both the East and the West, including "strategic" atomic weapons, is geared towards this ever-present possibility. Every one of these components of military preparedness must be present if deterrence is to be credible and to effectively preserve peace. Strangely enough, nobody questions the logic of this statement where "strategic" atomic weapons or armament on land and in the air are concerned. Doubts are voiced only with regard to the continued effectiveness of sea power as a means to control shipping routes. The reason given for this exception is that mastery of the sea—especially if the objective pursued by its exercise is economic—can be effective only if it has duration. The question whether sea power has any value in the nuclear age thus boils

[5] Here one may quote, among others, Vice Admiral Sir Peter Gretton, *Maritime Strategy, A Study of British Defense Problems* (Cassell, London, 1965), and L. W. Martin, *The Sea in Modern Strategy* (Chatto & Windus, London, 1967).

[6] Sir Julian Corbett agrees with Mahan (*Some Principles of Maritime Strategy*).

down to the further question whether a big war can conceivably last long enough for mastery of the sea or raider warfare to produce any significant results.

No doubt, if atomic strikes were ever exchanged, the "strategic" atomic phase would be relatively short, and while it lasted neither mastery of the sea nor raider warfare could play any major role. The destructive power of the atomic arsenal on both sides has today reached such terrifying proportions that both sides shy away most emphatically from the full application of its "strategic" atomic weapons. During this phase of restraint it could well be that by demonstrative use of atomic weapons—e.g., at sea, close to the enemy's territory—the parties are making clear their willingness to have recourse to this ultimate means, if the need arises. But this would be done precisely to prevent the big atomic spiral from being set in motion. If that deterrence is achieved, then the war in question would basically be a conventional war, even though tactical atomic weapons might be used during its course. A war of this nature could very well last over a longer period of time.

The naval armaments of the two world powers bear out this argument. Despite the umbrella of the atomic balance, both powers see the justification and the necessity for the existence of sea power in the possibility of an extended war. The majority of their naval forces are, therefore, conceived in the perspective of naval warfare in a traditional sense, i.e., warfare aimed at the protection or interruption of shipping routes, and by no means only in the perspective view of peacetime presence, crisis management, or limited action in the Third World, even though their forces can well be used in the framework of such activities.

No matter how one evaluates the possibility of "strategic" atomic restraint in a war between the two world powers, sea power and mastery of the sea retain their *political* relevance. The political effect of military armament has always depended on the possibility of its use in wartime. As far as naval armament is concerned this effect appears today bigger rather than smaller. Sea power is particularly suitable for giving impressive support to policies of overseas expansion. Without sea power, such expansion would not have a proper foundation. We will return to this aspect later on. Furthermore, the economic interdependence of all countries—and thereby, their dependence on the sea which, in wartime, means their dependence on that power which has mastery of the sea—is today greater than ever. For all these reasons, it would be just as inconceivable to exclude sea power from the catalogue of military instruments that the East needs to exert political pressure, as it would be for the West to omit it from its arsenal of deterrence.

The foregoing analysis of the pre-atomic phase does not cover the subject sufficiently. Despite the low degree of probability that atomic strikes will ever be exchanged, we have to examine the role that sea power would play in a post-atomic phase. It is, after all, a fact that the peace-preserving effect of "strategic" atomic armament is based on certain tenets which include assumptions as to what would happen if "strategic" atomic war should, all efforts notwithstanding, indeed come about.

One can safely assume that the party that first managed to rise again from the chaos of atomic destruction would have a decisive advantage in the continuation of the war. A premium in this post-atomic phase would thus at first be placed on restitution. Everything would depend on the speedy reconstruction of orderly life, the economy, and the military organization. If, in fact, nearly all resources in one's own country had been destroyed, the potential of the overseas world, so far left undamaged, would make more difference than ever. As none of the ships that had been at sea or in overseas ports during the atomic strike would have been affected, shipping could gradually be reorganized. But overseas resources could be used only by those who had mastery over the shipping routes. The other side would be excluded from this reservoir of vital resources. For the restitution phase, mastery of the sea—particularly, mastery of ocean areas—could thus be a decisive factor.

From a purely military point of view also mastery of the sea in the post-atomic phase would bring advantages. One can assume that the navies of both sides have survived to the extent that they were at sea at the time of the atomic strike. They might constitute the only military instrument ready for use at the moment. If land-based aviation, including the navy's, had been eliminated because its bases had been destroyed, carrier-based naval aviation could assume the highest importance. It could conceivably be the only aviation potential in existence. Carrier-based aircraft could thus be in a position to monopolize the air space above the sea and above the land, to the extent that land areas could be covered from the sea. If long-range "strategic" atomic weapons had been consumed on either side, carrier-based aircraft could well be the only remaining receptacles and sources of strategic nuclear arms.

Superior sea power, especially if it takes the form of a carrier-based air capability, could thus be a decisive factor not only at sea, but also on land, should the struggle be renewed. A belligerent party that was aware of its inferiority at sea, and knew that the enemy possessed advantages for continuing war after the exchange of atomic strikes, would be even more hesitant to decide in favor of an atomic strike in the first place. In this sense, sea power becomes an effective instrument of deterrence. It follows that, even under the auspices of the atomic balance, a long war in which sea power could be fully brought to bear is by no means impossible. The margin for the exercise of sea power is narrower than it was in former times, but its relative weight within this margin, and therefore its deterrent effect, have rather grown.

Atomic weapons and naval warfare

In connection with the preceding paragraphs, a few words must be said about "strategic" atomic weapons at sea and of the role of tactical atomic weapons in naval warfare.

When discussing the basic concepts of naval strategy, we did not mention the carriers of "strategic" atomic weapons at sea. The reason for this omission is that weapons systems of this nature—in spite of their eminent significance for overall strategy—do not have a role in naval warfare, properly speaking. Aircraft carriers play, in effect, a double role. When they are used to unleash an atomic strike they are to be judged by the criteria of nuclear strategy. Otherwise, they are part of the fleet, and engage in naval warfare. On the other hand, ships that are built exclusively for "strategic" atomic missions and armed correspondingly—as the Polaris submarine and its Soviet equivalent—are not suited for use in naval warfare. The targets for their weapons, ballistic-guided missiles, lie ashore, not at sea.

The commander of such a ship has no influence whatsoever on the choice of target or the time of firing. In fact, these decisions are not within the responsibility of the high command of naval operations, but are made by the central decision-making body for atomic strategy. Carriers of atomic weapons at sea are thus, strictly speaking, part of a nation's "strategic" atomic forces. In the U.S.S.R. these atomic forces even constitute a service of their own; the navy acts merely as a trustee. This trusteeship implies building and manning the ships, and then deploying them operationally. It is, however, a genuine naval task to *protect* these ships against enemy attack, and to *fight* the *enemy's* carriers of atomic weapons at sea.

It is commensurate with the eminent importance of "strategic" atomic weapons that the tasks relating to these carriers—be they genuine naval tasks, or implications of the trusteeship role—should consume a high proportion of the personnel and material capacity of the navy of an atomic power, and that a high priority be assigned to the corresponding activities. These tasks may well determine the composition of naval forces, and, even more, the entire structure of a navy.

Since the present study does not only deal with naval warfare as such, but with the role and significance of Soviet naval forces, it must include the Soviet Union's carriers of atomic weapons at sea and their equivalents in the West.

Tactical atomic weapons have a less incisive impact on naval war, than, relatively speaking, on land war. Naval forces can protect themselves sufficiently against atomic weapons by sailing in a well-spaced formation. Only one ship will be mortally hit by each atomic explosion. The incidental effects of atomic weapons will not materialize at sea. There are no populations to be exposed, no land areas to be polluted by radiation, and no destruction outside the military sphere. In contrast to a situation on land, where no clear line can be drawn between "strategic" and tactical atomic weapons, the use of tactical atomic weapons at sea—at least on the high seas—can hardly lead to a strategic atomic escalation. These facts have given rise to speculation as to whether a war between the superpowers could be totally, at least initially, fought at sea. However, since East and West depend on shipping to quite different degrees, an hypothesis of this nature does not appear very realistic.

Motives for using tactical atomic weapons at sea differ from those that prevail on land. At sea, recourse to tactical atomic weapons is not the last expedient for the losing party in an otherwise hopeless tactical or operational situation. Rather, use of tactical atomic weapons at sea can imply advantages—if also disadvantages—for both sides: surface ships are exposed to a higher risk. In view of the essential importance of American aircraft carriers for naval warfare in ocean areas, the U.S.S.R. would have a high-priority interest in using atomic weapons. On the other hand, the United States would be greatly interested in using atomic depth charges against submarines, especially submarines with atomic propulsion. Whether these differences in interest between East and West make for a balance that keeps both sides from using tactical atomic weapons at sea, is as yet an open question.

In any case, both sides are prepared to make an immediate change-over to using tactical atomic arms. Practically all ordnance is double-purpose, i.e., it can be used with both conventional and atomic ammunition. Ships on both sides carry atomic ammunition for these systems, even in peacetime. When the change-over for atomic weapons takes place, neither gradual escalation nor selective use is very likely. Under such circumstances, presumably all ordnance systems that are designed for atomic ammunition would be simultaneously devoted to such use.

Nuclear propulsion

In conclusion of our discussion of topics related to the atom, mention must be made of nuclear propulsion in ships. As is well known, ships so propelled can travel on the same fuel charge practically without time limitations and, what is more, can continuously run at top speed. As far as surface ships are concerned, these advantages do not bring about a complete change of scenario in a naval war theater. Because of their dependence on weather conditions, these ships can derive only a limited benefit from their ability to travel at top speed on a permanent basis. As long as there are, for economic reasons, only a few nuclear-propelled surface units—all of them on the U.S. side—nuclear ships are reduced to the limits of speed and endurance at sea of the conventional ships with which they are linked operationally. For this reason, a carrier task force, for instance, cannot do without afloat support during extended missions. Therefore, the increase in the operational mobility of nuclear-powered surface ships cannot be fully utilized at the present time.

For *nuclear-powered submarines* the situation is totally different. Since their propulsion system is not dependent on an outside oxygen supply, the characteristics of submarines change completely. Conventional submarines can proceed only slowly, because enemy air surveillance forces them to travel almost constantly in a submerged state while snorkeling. Only during attack or pursuit are they allowed to run at the top speed provided by their batteries—modest as that speed is compared to that of a nuclear submarine—and even that only for brief periods. Nuclear-powered submarines, by contrast, have considerably higher maximum speeds and can use them without limit and without regard to the motion of the sea.[7] With these features, their tactical and operationl possibilities are dramatically increased. The details of what that implies remain to be discussed at a latęr point. We will then see that the nuclear-powered submarine can in fact bring about a revolution in naval warfare.

Defense against nuclear-powered submarines

Considering these facts, we are immediately confronted with the question where the possibilities and limits for detecting and fighting nuclear-powered submarines lie. The problem becomes relevant in various contexts. It may therefore be appropriate to conclude this chapter with several basic, and some specific, comments on antisubmarine warfare (ASW).

Mastery of the sea relates only to the surface of the sea. It can be exercised only against surface ships. There is no such thing as mastery of subsurface waters, just as there is no mastery of the air space above the sea—unless, that is, the enemy's submarines or aircraft have been destroyed in their totality. Submarines and land-based aircraft, in their respective media, can easily intrude into the area where the adversary holds sea power. They can only be destroyed individually, one at a time.

Attack submarines that are stationed and remain outside the area where naval forces operate or where commercial shipping is carried on, are of no importance in naval war. However, if they stay in such an aloof position, they betray their mission. To fulfill it they must get close to their victims and have them within firing range. Then they have also entered into the

[7] Actual performances of nuclear-powered submarines are kept secret in both East and West. One can only state in a general way that the nuclear submarines of the U.S. Navy are faster and develop less noise than their Soviet counterparts.

underwater zone that ASW has to control. The longer the firing range of the submarine, the bigger the ASW zone and the more difficult the fulfillment of the ASW mission.[8]

The situation of submarines with a "strategic" atomic assignment is quite different. Their mission in fact requires an aloof posture that would make no sense for attack submarines: This proves once more that submarines with a strategic atomic task do not fall within the concept of sea power and cannot actively participate in naval warfare.

In our days, ASW technology relies almost totally on acoustics. Active and passive sonar devices, in part as dunking or variable-depth sonar for detecting submarines across layers of water impervious to sound, and antisubmarine (AS) torpedoes with a sonar head geared to specific submarine noises, are the main elements. Conventional submarines, with their relatively low speed, can be fought with considerable chances of success if these devices are employed from surface ships.

Chances of escape after detection grow proportionately with the submarine's available speed and with the depth it can attain. In these two respects, nuclear-powered submarines are vastly superior to conventional ones; and these are the main reasons why it is hardly possible for the established ASW technology to cover nuclear-powered submarines. Very advanced nuclear submarines feature, in addition, a lower noise level and more sensitive sensors. They can hear noises from other craft at ever-increasing distances and, at the same time, identify the type of vessel from which they stem. They themselves are heard only at ever-decreasing distances.[9] This means that nuclear-powered submarines can avoid ASW measures simply by making use of their superior speed as soon as they find that they have been detected. Thus, in the future, only those ASW measures that manage to detect without producing noise will be successful. The submarine must not know that it has been spotted.

[8] This is particularly true of submarines equipped with antiship missiles which enable them to attack from a submerged position over large distances and to remain far beyond the customary destroyer screen.

[9] In this "sensor race," destroyers, so far the mainstay of submarine-hunting operations, will be the losers. The faster they run, the noisier their screws, and their own sonar performance rapidly decreases with higher speeds. Also, since the modern nuclear-powered submarine is faster than the destroyer, the latter cannot pursue an escaping submarine. Newly designed or modernized destroyers, especially in Western navies, carry ASW helicopters. However, they usually carry only one or, at best, two.

This requirement is met by submarine-hunter helicopters equipped with passive dunking-sonar devices and passive sonar buoys. Under water, the submarine is not aware of the presence of a hunter helicopter. The latter's sonar devices are not affected by underwater noises of their own. Finally, the submarine-hunter helicopter can drop its AS weapons from the immediate proximity of the detected submarine.[10]

However, even the submarine-hunter helicopter does not completely solve the ASW problems connected with nuclear-powered submarines. Three of the several questions that remain to be answered are cited here:

1. The area around a task force or convoy that has to be covered is vast, particularly against submarines equipped with far-reaching torpedoes or—even more so—with antiship missiles. Each helicopter, however, can survey only a limited section. Since ASW searching has to be maintained around the clock, protection could be ensured only if helicopters were available in very large numbers. Destroyer-borne helicopters will never suffice.

2. Helicopters cannot stay with a rapidly advancing task force, unless search operations are to be constantly interrupted. Even an augmented number of helicopters can hardly guarantee the necessary defense of the task force, including the sea area ahead of the force.[11]

3. The cruising speed of even the most modern AS torpedoes is only slightly greater than that of fast nuclear submarines. When such a submarine is aware that a torpedo has been fired, it has a good chance to escape; the super-fast submarine of the future, whose speed may be equal to or even higher than that of an AS torpedo, will have a still better chance.

[10] Maritime Patrol Aircraft (MPA) operate along similar lines. Their principal mission is large-scale antisubmarine surveillance. When an MPA finds a submarine (for instance, by detecting its snorkel by radar or by infrared detector), unnoticed by the submarine it drops a sonar buoy. This buoy provides data on the submarine noise that allow its position to be marked and expose it to the use of AS torpedoes and depth charges.

[11] The problem of keeping pace with a rapidly advancing task force does not have to be faced by a submarine-hunting helicopter that is engaged in "stationary" submarine search. "Stationary" ASW is designed to cover busy intersections of oceanic traffic, areas adjacent to harbors and bases, and especially narrows through which submarines must pass on their way to their assigned area of operation. Stationary ASW can only be carried on in areas where one has control of the sea and of the air space above it.

It is not a rosy picture, then, that can be painted for the West in the ASW field in the face of steadily increasing numbers of Soviet nuclear-powered submarines. Tendencies in submarine construction clearly go in the direction of increased resistance against ASW measures. Increasingly, ASW cannot cope.

The only antisubmarine weapon that can be used from the surface with some chance of success even against very modern nuclear-powered submarines is the atomic depth charge. Modern surface ships are equipped with ordnance which, as well as conventional ASW devices, can fire atomic explosive devices over large distances. Given the huge perimeter of the effect of an atomic underwater explosion, even a super-fast submarine, vaguely spotted, can thus be affected. But, as we stated earlier, this atomic weapon would only be available at the price of far-reaching consequences for the further development of naval war.

We herewith conclude our general analysis of the basic concepts of naval strategy and of the conditions prevailing at sea in the nuclear age. The purpose of these general remarks will become clearer as they are put into perspective in the further course of this study. The results of our discussion can, as of now, be summarized as follows:

Even in the nuclear age and under the auspices of the atomic balance, the concepts of sea power and mastery of the sea retain their essential contents and their full significance. Atomic weapons, the nuclear-powered submarine, and other technical innovations will refashion the outer manifestations of naval war. However, in spite of all technological changes, the purpose and objective of naval war remains the double task of protecting one's own shipping, and preventing the enemy's transports from using the sea—in short, mastery of the sea.

2

from coastal defense to strategic naval offensive

The geographical situation

We are now ready to turn to the Soviet Union. Before we set out to examine the evolution of Soviet naval strategy, it is necessary to analyze briefly the geographical prerequisites for the formation of Russian sea power. The situation of Russia in relation to the sea is unfavorable in an almost grotesque manner. The original settlement area of the Russian people had no border on the sea at all. At present, the U.S.S.R. has a coastline extending more than 43,000 km. i.e., almost 28,000 miles. But in spite of this colossal stretch, the country—in relation to the size of its territory—is poorly endowed with suitable coasts. More than 90 percent of the coastline is so encumbered with ice that shipping is impossible, or possible only for short periods of the year.

To this handicap is added a second, even more important one: Russian territory is accessible to seagoing traffic only at four points that are separated by vast distances. Two of these points are situated on inland seas—the Baltic Sea and the Black Sea—whose entrances are not in Soviet hands. The other two points, on the Arctic Sea and in the Far East, are separated from the former, and also from each other, by huge distances. It is thus very difficult in wartime to unite forces from one position with those of another, and even impossible in the face of an enemy who has mastery of the oceans. In saying this, let us neglect for the moment the possibility of the Arctic Sea fleet and the Baltic fleet uniting after the Baltic approaches had been forced open. Artificial waterways, like the White Sea Canal, which links the Baltic and Arctic seas, and the river and canal system between the Don, Volga, and Baltic Sea, do not remedy this geographical separation. Ice closes these waterways for long periods and numerous locks impede shipping. The dimensions of the locks, the clearance of bridges, and the water depths available are insufficient for the transfer of surface ships of a certain size, and even of large submarines. The Northern Passage, which can only be used during a few weeks in summer, does not constitute a suitable link in an East-West conflict, because its final leg, the Bering Strait, passes immediately opposite the U.S. coast off Alaska. Only the naval air arm and, to some extent, submarines can overcome the handicap of geographical separation in wartime.

However, it is not only the facts that the four areas are spread so far apart and that the Soviet Navy is divided up in four different fleets that make Russia's naval strategic-geographical position appear so unfavorable. Another difficulty is that all four positions are either entirely cut off from or far removed from the oceans. In order to reach for the ocean, all four fleets must pass through narrows of various widths that can easily be placed under enemy surveillance. In the radar age, even the sea area between Scotland and Iceland appears as a narrows, at least for surface ships.

Separation of the four Soviet strategic positions and the four Soviet fleets from one another and generally their recessed locations in relation to the ocean are the basic features of Soviet naval strategy, as they were in the past. In a way, our discussion centers around whether and how the U.S.S.R. could—by armament or by advancing its position in the course of military or political expansion—overcome the disadvantages of its geographical situation under circumstances of global confrontation with Western sea power, an adversary with such obvious geographical advantages.

Russian sea power in history

The Russian Navy can look back upon almost 300 years of history. In spite of this considerable lapse of time, the Soviet

Navy of today is young in terms of naval strategy. For its modern history, properly speaking, started only about 20 years ago when it reached a turning-point of utmost significance. We do not know at exactly what date that point was reached or even whether the turn was the result of a rationally conceived long-term strategic plan. But an important change has come about. We will soon recognize its dimensions.

Whether it was a conscious act of revolution or not, it is a fact that Russian naval strategy, from its beginning and then without interruption up to the era that came to an end 20 years ago, was based on the same doctrine—a doctrine that can be characterized as the "battleship concept." Peter the Great and Catherine embraced that concept in their time. In the limitations of the two internal seas, the Baltic Sea and the Black Sea, and against the competitors there, Sweden on the one hand, the Ottoman Empire on the other, that concept was perfectly appropriate. The political objective of extending Russian might to the Baltic countries and to the Ukraine, required the formation of sea power. In the Baltic Sea this implied, in addition, creating a naval strategic position, something the Russians had so far lacked entirely. The foundation of St. Petersburg, an artificially created city at the only point where Russia bordered on the Baltic at that time, thus appears to have been an act of strategic naval offensive. Russia finally became the dominant naval power in both these internal seas.

When the Turkish Navy was in its decline and the Scandinavian states fell back to a second-rank position, the danger arose that Russia, without a potent naval counterweight, would transform the two internal seas into "closed seas." The European powers took political steps against a naval hegemony of this order, and saw to it that the narrows that provided access to the two internal seas did not fall into Russian hands. Their intention was to ensure that the two seas remained open for trade and, in war and peace, for the naval forces of non-riparian states. That these policies have remained successful up to the present time is manifest in Denmark's and Turkey's membership in NATO.

Coinciding with these developments, the center of gravity of world sea traffic changed from the peripheral seas of Europe to the oceans. Both facts together produced the effect that the Russian fleets lost their political weight. Russian sea power did not extend beyond the narrows. Her fleets were reduced to the mission of coastal defense. Even for this defensive task they were not particularly well suited, since Russia lacked the means to maintain in all her separate naval districts naval forces strong enough to withstand an invader in a battle at sea. This became evident in the Black Sea in the Crimean War, and in the Baltic when the German fleet was confronted in the First World War. Russia's unsuccessful attempt, after the elimination of her Far Eastern fleet in the Russo-Japanese War, to tilt the power balance in her favor in the Sea of Japan by moving her Baltic fleet around the globe, only emphasizes the perennial predicament that results from the "basic pattern" of her geographically spread-out positions.

However, Czarist Russia need not have resigned herself to that predicament. At least from the turn of the century onward, technological development offered new weapons for defense in coastal areas—at first mines, torpedo boats, and long-range coastal artillery, then submarines, and finally aircraft. The position from which such weapons systems can be brought to direct use—the coast—thereby gains in factor value. The factor fleet can then remain small in terms of the combat value of individual units, especially if the fleet is numerous. The result could be coastal sea power not only sufficient but even particularly suited for defense. In other words, in coastal areas the smaller instruments of naval warfare may establish sufficient mastery of the sea to ensure that shipping routes in one's own coastal area remain under one's own control and are closed to the enemy. For Russia, a coastal defense of this sort would have been more efficient and more economical than defense by battleships. Czarist Russia lacked the insight to understand this. As did other European powers of the time, she saw powerful squadrons of battleships as an attribute of big-power status, without regard to geography or to the strategic mission of the ships. Thus, even after the defeat at Tsushima, Russia clung to the battleship concept as if this were a matter of course. At great sacrifice and in the shortest possible time a new and even stronger battleship fleet was built in the Baltic. It was still under construction when the war broke out in 1914.

Developments after the October Revolution

It is rather astonishing that the Russian Revolution which brought about a "revaluation of all values" in so many other fields, did not effect any change in the field of naval strategy. But it is an indisputable fact that Lenin, and later, in an even more pronounced fashion, Stalin steadfastly held on to traditional battleship thinking in spite of the triple failure of the inherited doctrine. There is no point in trying to guess why they did so; perhaps it was with a view to their ultimate objective of socialist world domination, in which case their analysis of naval strategic conditions was definitely faulty; or perhaps they believed—as did the Czars—that battleships represented power as such. One can at least make the following statement: neither of them had a "sea-oriented" mentality, or distinguished himself by logically consistent naval strategic thinking.

Lenin was unable in the aftermath of revolutionary turmoil and civil war to build a modern battleship fleet—he limited himself to the restitution of old battleships and cruisers from the Czarist Navy—and that task fell to his successor. As soon as industrial capacity, barely recovered from the destructions of war time, permitted, Stalin twice ordered the construction of fleets that strike us as gigantic. The first time, in 1938, super-sized battleships were to be the mainstay of naval forces. The second time, in the framework of the construction program of 1950 and according to the lessons that were drawn from the Pacific war, not battleships, but destroyers and cruisers were emphasized, the latter to attain 15,000 tons. In a second construction phase, aircraft carriers were included.[12] This element of Stalin's second naval constructon program is especially astonishing if we consider the fact that such carriers were presumably also ordered for the Baltic and the Black Sea, narrow sea areas that are much more easily covered by land-based naval aviation.

Especially after the Second World War, the construction of these surface ships was accompanied by the construction of a submarine fleet. This part of Soviet naval planning was indeed opportune. It is no coincidence that after Stalin's death the submarine fleet could be integrated smoothly into the new Soviet concept of naval strategy.

Even if Stalin's fleets of surface ships had been built according to their time schedule, they would have had no global political effect, in spite of their colossal dimensions. Without geographical positions outside their own territorial waters, these

[12] Cf. R. W. Herrick, *Soviet Naval Strategy* (U.S. Naval Institute, Annapolis, 1968).

fleets would have been reduced, as were their predecessors, to the status of coastal defense forces.

The "turn" after Stalin's death

Stalin's death in 1953 brought his naval construction program to a halt. His disappearance from the scene marks the "turn" we referred to above. Hardly had he been buried, when the independent Ministry of the Navy was abolished. The Navy then came under the Ministry of Defense. There, the Army marshals were in firm command. They had looked with extreme dislike upon Stalin's preference for the Navy. If they had had their way, the Navy would have been abolished altogether, or at least made into a mere auxiliary force of the Army. In their thinking, the age-old Russian continental mentality which had always tended to consider the fleet an unnecessary luxury, came to the fore. Even Marshal Sokolovsky, the highly considered Soviet strategist, in his book *Military Strategy* bothers to enumerate only those functions that the Navy can perform to support activities of the Army. Only in a marginal way does he concede: "Although these are not the only tasks the navy has to fulfill, a substantial part of the navy must be allocated to them." And still in 1964 he writes in an article: "Only the firing of rockets from submarines gives to the navy a function of its own in far-away ocean areas. Nothing else must divert it from its principal task in war which is to operate along the coast in close collaboration with army troops." In the view of the Army strategists, the Navy was to be the "faithful servant of the army," and nothing else. This detail is included here to show how far away from a sea-oriented mentality many circles in the U.S.S.R. still were at the time. It also illustrates the extraordinary nature of the evolution that took place shortly thereafter.

The first step after Stalin's death was an order to stop shipbuilding at once. Next came an order to scrap all larger surface ships. However, this latter order was executed by the Navy only reluctantly and halfheartedly. In reality, the only ships that were scrapped were the few old battleships that dated from before the First World War and had become totally useless anyway, with some outdated cruisers thrown in. The newly appointed high command of the Soviet Navy under Admiral Gorshkov also managed to circumvent the first one of the two orders. Not only were those cruisers and destroyers that had been built and commissioned under the Stalin program maintained in active service, but an additional 14 cruisers from the program were completed. Besides, there was some confusion among Soviet leaders as to what to do with the Navy at this point. In the course of their discussions some weight was given to the argument that surface ships had basically become obsolete in the era of nuclear armament. No matter how the debate went in detail throughout its almost two years of duration, one thing was certain from the outset: a radical departure from Stalin's concept of naval armament as a preparation for the battle at sea was to be the result. Despite strong opposition from inside the party, and despite Khrushchev's initial reluctance, it was finally decided to resume naval construction. However, the fleet was to consist of small units only, and especially of submarines.

There is a strange contradiction between these decisions and the fact that the Navy took advantage of the abruptly imposed building stop to have amphibious craft constructed and launched! And another surprising development is worth mentioning: before the fifties drew to a close the newly ordered concept with its dislike of powerful surface ships was again abandoned. Suddenly, we see the beginning of the well-known construction phase of large destroyers and cruisers, both equipped with ship-to-ship missiles—a development that was hardly in keeping with the small-unit concept. Strangely enough, Gorshkov defended these types before the Communist Party Congress by saying that they were indispensable for escorting submarines to the Iceland-Scotland narrows, and that, in addition, they represented something diametrically opposed to all former surface ships.

Looking back on this phase of Soviet naval policy, we do not have the impression of a well-conceived, consistent, long-term naval concept. It is too early to know whether such a strategic concept perhaps existed in the minds of individual leaders who succeeded only gradually in imposing their views in the face of strong opposition. We can only say that sometime after Stalin's death there occurred the "turning point," which implied abandonment of his battleship concept.[13]

[13] In depicting events after Stalin's death our main source was Herrick, *op. cit.* Later authors do not always agree with Herrick's description. It is now being pointed out, with good reason, that it would have been

Naval strategy after the "turn"

In view of the naval superiority of NATO, the U.S.S.R. after Stalin's death again had to take "coastal defense" for a starting point. At first, the construction program for missile ships therefore reflected a continuation of the previous strategic naval defensive. The later notion of a naval offensive was at that point only cautiously intimated by the construction of amphibious forces. The new elements consisted merely in the slightly changed tactical concept of attrition of the assailant by the instruments of "small war." The objective would not be a decisive victory in the "battle at sea" but a series of individual actions in which the aggressor would have to eliminate an accumulation of various naval forces at a substantial loss to himself. Thus, in this first phase after the "turn," the basic scenario was a classical coastal defense strategy, as described above.

However, this defensive concept was soon transformed by a highly significant shift in emphasis. When the United States assigned to its aircraft carriers an atomic role in the framework of the doctrine of "massive retaliation" (the first carrier of the *Forrestal* class was commissioned in 1955), Soviet territory was exposed to a threat far more dangerous than any that had ever emanated from the possibility of enemy invasion. By necessity, Soviet naval defense centered around arming against this nuclear peril.

In fact, the peril threatened from all directions of the compass: from the Norwegian Sea, from the North Sea, from the Eastern Mediterranean, and also from the Northern Pacific. Obviously, it was necessary to build naval forces that would be

impossible to embark on the construction of missile destroyers and cruisers in the late 1950s if the green light came only after lengthy inner-party discussion in the aftermath of Stalin's death. One must assume rather that decisions were taken much earlier, probably when Stalin was still alive. In that case, the pause in construction would have rather been caused by technical difficulties in the transition from the old construction program to the new, and had nothing to do with political debates about the Navy. From this correction of the more accepted picture of the construction process, one may not, however, infer that Stalin had changed his strategic naval concept. The new types of ships could very well be accommodated in the framework of his views, just as they fitted into the new concept. This interpretation has the advantage of assuming a greater degree of continuity in the naval construction program than is apparent from Herrick's description.

able to confront and attack the carriers before they reached their starting points. If even some of these carriers could be destroyed, damaged, or made to turn away, then nuclear destruction within the country could at least be minimized. The Soviet naval leadership was thus forced to extend its defensive effort towards the areas from which a naval threat might come, and thereby went beyond the needs of mere coastal defense.

The necessity to cover large new areas became particularly evident in a new concept for the naval air arm. In the Stalin era naval aviation consisted largely of fighter squadrons. Its mission was to defend naval bases and to provide air cover for Soviet naval forces close to the coasts. Under the new concept, these fighter squadrons were reassigned to domestic air defense. They were replaced by medium-range bombers suited for combat above the open sea. Gradually, these bombers were armed with highly effective, long-range, stand-off type air-to-ship missiles. The zone of defense could then be widened to the limits of their range of operation. The result was a geographically advanced naval defense with a triple-wave system that included missile-armed bomber planes, surface ships that were likewise armed with missiles, and submarines for defensive purposes. This concept of defense by three successive "waves" can easily be deduced from the pattern of Soviet naval exercises, especially those that take place in the Norwegian Sea.

In direct proportion with the rapid growth of Soviet forces, this system of defending large sea areas has achieved a high degree of effectiveness in all four Soviet naval districts. As the system becomes even more accomplished, the Soviets increasingly acquire the means to shift from a defensive naval strategy to a partially offensive one. Thus they are able to question the West's mastery of the sea, which has heretofore been undisputed even in areas off the Soviet coasts. Owing to this naval strategy of the Soviets, the Western powers would—in wartime—be able to cruise in these sea areas only at substantial risk. But if the West avoided these areas altogether, it would virtually cede them to the Soviets: it would be able to manifest itself only with submarines, an implied admission of Soviet mastery of the sea. The Soviets have achieved this remarkable feat without improving their geographical position—merely by making full use of modern technical means, which is to say, in terms of the concepts developed here, by strengthening their factor "fleet."

It appears that the Soviets have thus solved the problem of

protecting their coasts. The fact that it is now the neighboring NATO countries who find themselves forced to establish a system of coastal defense, after a long period in which their coasts were protected by Western mastery of the sea, makes the Soviet switch to the offensive quite apparent. For the objective of Soviet mastery of the sea in these areas is not so much the free use of shipping routes for economic reasons. It is military in nature. The Soviets' aim is to advance their naval strategic positions in order to expand the sea area under their control even farther towards the enemy. This is clearly a strategic naval offensive, an offensive that has already largely achieved its first objective—mastery of the sea in areas adjacent to their own territory.

The degree of mastery of the sea that the Soviets have now obtained is certainly not absolute. It is limited in terms of time and space. If the West managed to intrude into one of the areas covered by the new Soviet concept, and to sojourn there, Soviet mastery of the sea would, theoretically, be suspended in that area.

Strategic atomic threat at sea

Let us now return briefly to the initial Soviet motive in expanding coastal defenses: the strategic atomic threat presented by U.S. aircraft carriers. In spite of the important consequences for naval strategy that resulted from its original anti-carrier concept, whose motivation was in nuclear strategy, the Soviet Union has not attained its goal of protecting its territory against the seaborne atomic potential of the West. This is because carriers had lost their mission of executing the strategic strike against first-priority targets—and thus their strategic atomic role proper—before the Soviet Union had fully implemented its anti-carrier concept. The mission to execute strategic strikes devolved upon the Polaris submarines. From the standpoint of purely nuclear strategy, the Soviet Union completely missed its objective by adopting the anti-carrier concept.

As the nature of the strategic atomic threat changed, the Soviets found themselves *vis-à-vis* a completely different situation. Instead of defense against aircraft carriers, the strategic atomic situation called for defense against Polaris submarines. Since then, the predominant theme in Soviet naval construction has been the antisubmarine concept. However, the anti-carrier mission has not been abandoned. Only the reasoning behind it has changed: it is now a matter of naval, not atomic, strategy. It remains an important element of Soviet naval strategy and has been surpassed in emphasis only by the antisubmarine concept.

In order to meet the newly recognized threat, the Soviets gave priority to the development of ASW systems, an area in which they had been technologically behind. They made good progress in ASW techniques both from surface ships and from the air. As advanced ASW equipment became ready for use, the design of Soviet destroyers and cruisers of recent construction increasingly bore the imprint of the ASW mission. Now, these units can almost be referred to as huge ASW craft. The latest—and belated—offspring of these efforts are the two helicopter carriers of the *Moskva* class, specially outfitted to carry submarine-hunter helicopters.

Hardly had the Soviets reaped the first fruits of their investments in this field, when the Polaris submarines began to extract themselves from these dangers. Stationary, systematic ASW from surface ships—directly or with the aid of helicopters—is possible in wartime only in sea areas where one exercises mastery of the sea. When the firing range of their ballistic missiles increased, it became possible for the Polaris submarines to vacate their positions in Soviet-controlled sea areas, notably in the Arctic Sea, and to stay in ocean areas where the West possesses mastery of the sea. Again, a powerful Soviet attempt to stave off a weapons system that carries strategic atomic weapons failed to attain its target.

But even though the original goal was missed, the Soviet Navy can credit itself with a valuable side-effect of its efforts. Just as the anti-carrier concept, which was introduced on a strategic atomic motive, liberated it from a narrow view of coastal defense, endowed it with a full-fledged high seas fleet, and gave it mastery in the peripheral seas, so did the anti-Polaris concept enable it to catch up in ASW technology, so far neglected, and to build up an ASW capability for these peripheral seas that commands respect.

On the basis of the foregoing, we will now try to assess in greater detail the impact these developments have had in each of the peripheral seas that form the Soviet Union's naval districts.

3

the role of soviet naval forces in peripheral seas

The Norwegian Sea

Of the four sea areas adjacent to Soviet territory, the Norwegian Sea, as the European part of the Arctic Ocean, is the most important from a naval strategic standpoint. It is connected with the Atlantic Ocean. The Scotland-Iceland narrows separate the two sea areas but, at the same time, they provide access to the Atlantic and constitute a gateway through which—by comparison with the other three sea areas—Soviet naval forces can most easily and most directly reach the ocean. On the other hand, Western sea power exercises its threat at this very gateway. If Western naval forces decided to forge into the Norwegian Sea, their primary route would be through these narrows. Murmansk, on the Kola Peninsula, is situated in almost the farthest eastern corner, beyond the North Cape—not even on the Norwegian Sea, but on the Barents Sea. The Soviet naval strategic position could hardly be less advantageously placed.

Any strategic mission, be it defensive or offensive, must therefore generate in Soviet naval leadership the urge to improve this position. Since that can be done only at Norway's expense, by strategic necessity, we must impute to the Soviet Union the aim of including all or part of Norway into its realm of power, if possible by political means but, if not, by military might. We are here concerned with the military threat.

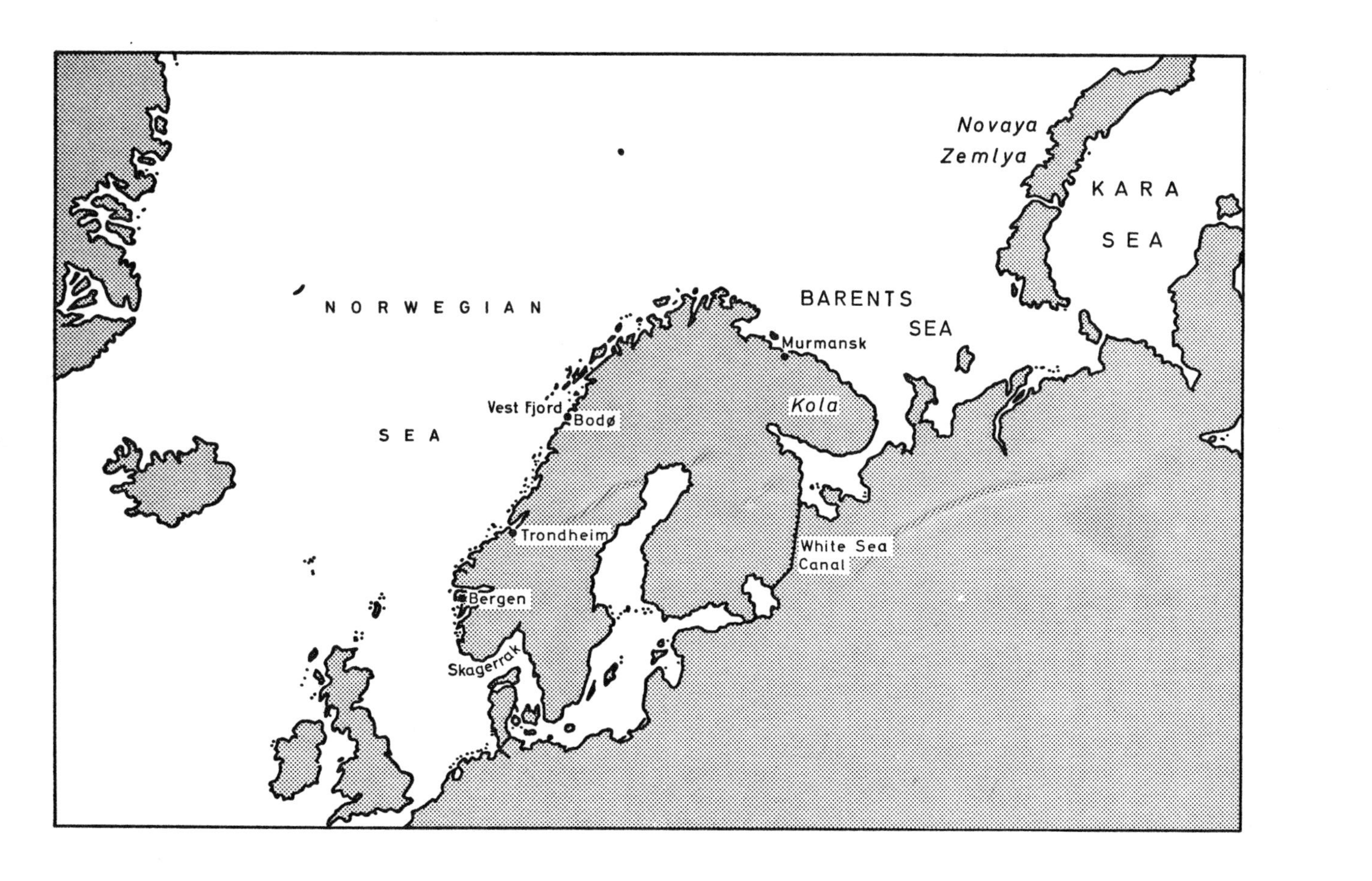
Novaya
Zemlya
KARA
SEA
NORWEGIAN
SEA
BARENTS
SEA
Murmansk
Kola
Vest Fjord
Bodø
Trondheim
White Sea
Canal
Bergen
Skagerrak

The threat to northern Norway

In the first place, northern Norway is subject to that threat. NATO plans are oriented towards the defense of that area. Although all branches of Norway's armed forces are concentrated there, forceful NATO support is needed. Secure sea lanes along the Norwegian coast are a prerequisite of such support. In addition, the Norwegians count on the West to assist them in their fight on land, primarily with carrier-based aircraft which could most rapidly bring tactical atomic weapons to bear in an area otherwise kept free from nuclear weapons on the NATO side. The deterrent effect of such potential intervention is an essential element in Norway's NATO membership.

Unfortunately, it is open to doubt whether the troops required for the effective defense of northern Norway on land and in the air could be made available and, even more important, could be moved there in time. Thus, the defense of the area depends essentially on timely support by aircraft carriers. It is conceivable that northern Norway would have to be abandoned down to a point narrow enough to be blocked off and defended more easily. However, if that were to happen, the overall naval strategic situation of the West would thereupon be substantially diminished. The Soviets could advance their position for naval warfare around the North Cape and southward.

Not only northern Norway, but all Norway is likewise threatened—first, central Norway, then western Norway. Geographic factors make rapid occupation of these areas by land from the north impossible; there is only one road. Occupation by air alone is equally impossible. Because of the limited capacity of Norwegian airfields, the supply problem could not be solved by air transport alone. Occupation, then, would have to take place primarily from the sea. With the exception of Bodø and a few fjords that are protected by artillery, Norway's coastline south of Vest Fjord is virtually undefended. A Soviet *coup de main* against these coasts (possibly during or even before fighting in northern Norway) can thus not be excluded. If the Soviets had free access by sea to their northern bases, they could relatively quickly consolidate a bridgehead position by redeploying naval air squadrons, concentrating coastal defense forces (particularly missile-equipped fast patrol boats [FPB], antiair and antiship missile batteries) at the new location, and making arrangements for seaborne supply.

NATO operations in the Norwegian Sea

A Soviet invasion of northern Norway can be prevented or countered only if the West continues to possess mastery of the sea and of the air space above it. Let us assume that the West clearly recognized a threat and decided to take effective preventive action: it would then be only logical to dispatch a powerful naval task force to the Norwegian Sea, at the very latest when the war broke out.

A Western task force, which would need a nucleus of aircraft carriers, would certainly be spotted by the adversary's reconnaissance as it approached through the northern Atlantic. While passing through the Scotland-Iceland narrows it would be in the area where Soviet missile bombers threaten. The risk created by this "first wave" of possible attack would be high, especially if tactical nuclear warheads were likely to be employed. Thereafter the risk would become even higher as the task force approached Soviet naval air bases—not to mention the risk it would take by prolonging its stay within the proximity of those bases. The Western aircraft carriers' capability for self-defense in the face of bombers equipped with stand-off missiles is presently unsatisfactory. The forthcoming introduction of the F-14 with its new air-to-air missile system, Phoenix, which features improved performance and operational radius will increase this capability in the near future. In bomber-infested areas, some aircraft of the F-14 type can stay permanently above the carrier and open fire on attacking bomber planes—even on several simultaneously—long before the latter come within their missile-launching range. As has so often been the case in the history of weapons development, we observe an exciting race between defensive and offensive weapons systems. Bombers carrying stand-off missiles were the reply to antiair missiles. The response to that challenge is the air-to-air missile of superior radius: its use in the open seas, however, depends on the presence of aircraft carriers.

Greater significance must be attached—especially with a glance towards the future—to the "second wave," i.e., to the deployment of Soviet submarines across a broad front reaching from the Scotland-Iceland gap to the Norwegian coast. As long as the greater part of the Soviet defensive submarine force consists of conventionally propelled boats, the danger that emanates from it is still in a lower range than that created by the "first wave." In each case, only those submarines passed by the adversary's task force at a fairly close distance can see action. The same holds true of submarines equipped with ship-to-ship missiles. Against conventional submarines, the defensive screen established by escort destroyers proves rather effective. However, as soon as the "second wave" consists predominantly of nuclear-powered submarines, that situation will change. In sharp contrast with conventional subs, nuclear submarines with their high underwater cruising speed can operate in the direction of the reported enemy task force. The operational possibility for nuclear-powered submarines to stalk up to a carrier force, even from a substantial distance, increases in proportion to the length of its stay off Norway's coast.

The defensive effect of the "third wave"—missile cruisers and missile destroyers—should be calculated at a lesser rate, in spite of the range of its ship-to-ship missiles and the increase in impact and efficiency of surface-to-air missile systems aboard. The air power of aircraft carriers is still superior to that of surface ships of this kind. This will be especially true when the U.S. Navy possesses, as will soon be the case, air-to-ship missiles that permit stand-off attack upon Soviet cruisers and destroyers from outside the effective range of the latter's antiair missiles.

It becomes clear from these facts that a big Western task force, complete with carriers, would be able to advance into the Norwegian Sea in wartime, albeit at substantial risk. However, it could hardly dare to plan on a prolonged sojourn, especially in sea areas adjacent to Soviet bases. In addition, there is considerable doubt that such a task force could arrive in time, in case of a surprise Soviet move.

The situation in the Norwegian Sea

We must conclude that the menace to Norway is genuine. It is an indication of the fact that the Soviets have been successful in carrying their naval strategic offensive into the European part of the Arctic Ocean. They are now reaping the fruits of their attempt to establish sea power in the Norwegian Sea, notwithstanding the fact that their initial motive was one of purely nuclear strategy. As in all other Soviet naval districts, the gained extension of sea power rests solely upon the factor fleet, whose rapid construction is particularly suited, technically and numerically, to the geographic and naval strategic conditions in this sea area. The model of the "three waves" comes out very neatly in the overall design and deployment of Soviet forces in the Norwegian Sea.

It must be acknowledged that, so far, the West has not done anything of significance to defend against this Soviet naval strategic offensive. In the more than ten years during which the Soviets built up their sea power in the Norwegian Sea, the factor fleet on the Western side remained barely constant. The West continues to rely upon its carriers and their own protective equipment, upon the antiair and antisubmarine defense of escort destroyers, and upon the effectiveness of carrier aircraft, even in the face of surface units equipped with powerful antiair missiles. In spite of the many improvements in weapons development, this level of armament would not allow a Western carrier task force to eliminate quickly the numerous submarines and missile-equipped bomber aircraft that threaten it. Since it could not expose itself to continued Soviet assaults for any extended period, a Western naval operation in the Norwegian Sea could not be anything but a sortie into enemy territory. Before the Western task force appeared, and after its retreat, mastery of the sea would belong to the Soviets.

The deficiencies of Western sea power in the area include position. Since the purpose is to protect Norway from surprise attacks, the West would stand a chance only if it could operate from a position that was more advantageous in relation to the sea area in question than was the position of the Soviets. It is evident that the American east coast is not a satisfactory position in this context. Even the fjords of Scotland, including Scapa Flow, are too remote. Only a position on the Norwegian coast itself would be fully satisfactory. This would require some of the Norwegian fjords to be equipped as harbors to provide shelter for Western naval forces against submarine and aircraft attack, and to serve as a base from which those forces could intervene at any time. In a crisis situation, strong forces would have to be located in the fjords, unless—even better—a force of the necessary caliber could be permanently stationed in the Norwegian Sea, as the Sixth Fleet is in the Mediterranean. Such an arrangement would have a double deterrent effect: on the one hand, because of its inherent military potential; on the other, because a Soviet attack upon Norway would immediately bring the United States into the struggle.

However, whether it would be possible to keep the situation

under control, even with the aid of such measures, is uncertain. Although protection against air attacks would become more effective, the expected increase in numbers of Soviet nuclear submarines would render the deployment of aircraft carriers in relatively narrow waters like the Norwegian Sea more and more risky. One might well ask whether the defense of Norway could not be achieved more rationally by copying from the Soviets. To do so, the West would have to earmark nuclear submarines for the Norwegian Sea and build additional airfields in Norway, to which NATO's land-based naval aviation forces could be ordered on short notice. This kind of construction work would greatly increase the factor value of the Norwegian position. Unfortunately, there is not as yet the slightest sign that such prophylactic defense measures are being taken.

Let us summarize: NATO's situation in the Norwegian Sea gives rise to serious concern. Especially would the loss of western Norway—and then, necessarily, of southern Norway—have the gravest consequences in terms of naval strategy and overall strategy. The defense of the Danish narrows, which would then be menaced from either side, could hardly be guaranteed for any substantial length of time. The Soviet Northern Fleet could conceivably unite with the Soviet Baltic Fleet at the western Norwegian position. The realm of Soviet mastery of the sea would thus be extended into the North Sea. Access routes to the Atlantic would be substantially shortened for Soviet submarines.

It is hardly necessary to describe in detail the political and strategic consequences of such events for central Europe. The unfortunate situation in the Norwegian Sea is not only a result of dramatically increased Soviet armament since the "turn." It is just as much a result of the weakness of the West. One must refer specifically to the decline of British sea power, since the Norwegian Sea originally fell within the British sphere of responsibility in the NATO framework.

The naval strategic situation in the Baltic

In the Baltic, too, the enormous increase in Soviet naval armament has brought about Soviet mastery of the sea, based upon a naval strategic position that reaches from Finland all the way to the city gates of Lubeck. As far as the island of Bornholm it is virtually undisputed. In times of conflict, the West would be unable to enter the area with surface ships; only submarines and naval aircraft could be used east of Bornholm. NATO contests the Soviet claim to mastery of the sea only in the area west of the island. Just as in the Norwegian Sea, one must impute to the Soviets an offensive strategy in the Baltic, a strategy aimed at further expansion. Clearly, in the wake of age-old Russian dreams of power, it covets control of the Baltic approaches and thereby of absolute and complete control of the Baltic area. The Baltic, in the Soviet view, is to become their *mare clausum*. Control of the Baltic approaches means the inclusion of Denmark in the Soviet power sphere. If political attempts at such inclusion should fail, then occupation in wartime must be considered.

German and Danish observers saw Soviet naval armament as the expression of a strategic offensive even when the NATO view was that overall Soviet naval strategy had to be defined as defensive. For some considerable time now, the official NATO doctrine also holds that Soviet naval strategy in the Baltic constitutes an offensive. Today, the significance of the Danish narrows and the devastating effects on overall strategy that the loss of that position would have on the defense of all central and northern Europe, are quite clearly recognized. Soviet naval strategy aims at liberating its Baltic naval potential, now blocked off by the Danish narrows, at advancing the Soviet position to the Skagerrak, and then—as an alternative or as a supplementary measure to its offensive in the Norwegian Sea—at taking possession of southern Norway from the south.

The Soviet Baltic Fleet

The Soviet Union has reached its present power position at sea in the Baltic by applying, again, its "three wave" doctrine. The missile bombers of the Soviet Baltic Fleet constitute the "first wave." Their principal mission is to fight any U.S. carriers that advance into the North Sea. In the original concept, their mission was, again, designed to repel a strategic nuclear attack. As in the Norwegian Sea, that threat has ceased to exist. Defense against strategic nuclear submarines is not a problem here either. But their mission to attack carriers has not undergone any change; the Soviets attach high importance to preventing outside support in the form of carrier-borne aircraft from backing NATO defenses in the Baltic. Such support would, as in the Norwegian

Sea, not only strengthen local NATO forces in a general way, but would bring in the nuclear element. Neither NATO naval forces in the Baltic, nor Denmark's defense forces have tactical nuclear arms. In an atom-free zone the Soviet Union can hope first to seize the coveted strategic objective without setting in motion the nuclear danger spiral. The use of American carrier aircraft would directly involve the United States and make that Soviet calculation obsolete. The mission of the "first wave," then, is very well reasoned.

A carrier task force in the central or northern North Sea would face a serious threat from Soviet missile bombers. It would also have to consider the possibility of submarine attacks. The situation is substantially similar to that of a carrier in the Norwegian Sea; a prolonged sojourn in the proximity of the Baltic theater has become impossible. A Western aircraft carrier force would, therefore, probably attempt brief sorties to remain outside the firing range of Soviet missile bombers and in waters shallow enough to eliminate the risk of submarines, for example, at the southern entrance to the English Channel or at a position west of England. Distance to the target area would thus increase, and the effectiveness of carrier aircraft missions would diminish. Although this is an important argument, it is less important than the crucial question whether support from carrier aircraft could be present at all in time to influence the decision in the Baltic.

Obviously, Soviet missile bombers are likely to be employed also within the Baltic area itself. To use long-range missiles, which are designed for big surface-ship targets, against small craft is hardly economical. This is particularly true when these small vessels cruise in interior Danish waters or remain close to land. In proximity to the coast, the missile's homing device will not function. Big NATO units cruising in an open-sea area, on the other hand, would incur a high risk. Moreover, small craft would be vulnerable to the sorties of fighter-bomber aircraft from airfields in the area of Mecklenburg and Pomerania, although these aircraft are not specifically armed for such targets.

The "second wave," the submarine wave, has lost importance in the Baltic. Soviet submarines, it is true, contribute their share to making it impossible for the West to enter the eastern Baltic with surface ships, but in those sea areas in which NATO naval forces predominantly fulfill their defense mission, the risk of a submarine attack can be all but disregarded. This is so because the Soviet Union has scrapped its small, outmoded submarines without replacing them. For submarines with a 1,000-ton displacement (now the smallest type of Soviet submarine) at least Mecklenburg Bay and Kiel Bay are too shallow. Considering their limited task, the number of Soviet submarines in the Baltic appears somewhat out of proportion. It is possible that it is kept so big for training assignments in peace, and not so much for assignments in war. Probably part of the submarine fleet would be removed from the Baltic even before the outbreak of hostilities. As a result, ASW no longer commands first priority for NATO naval forces in the Baltic.

The significance of the "third wave," surface ships, is so much the higher. The Soviet high command could hardly delay its offensive operations until after NATO naval forces had been destroyed and sea lanes leading to NATO coasts had been completely secured. If an invasion were planned, amphibious forces would have to be moved sooner than that. They need cover. In contrast to the situation in the Norwegian Sea, the "third wave" constitutes the essential part of the Soviet Baltic Fleet. But even taking that fact into account, the naval forces of the Soviet Baltic Fleet must be rated as proportionately overstrong. Especially the modern missile cruisers and missile destroyers are too big for operations in the Baltic, where they are particularly exposed to mines, missile-carrying German aircraft, and FPBs. Their tasks could very well be taken over by smaller missile-equipped units. It thus appears that the deployment of the missile cruiser/destroyer force in the Baltic is somewhat out of proportion to the inherent risks. It is conceivable that these units are retained in the Baltic only because the supreme command counts upon a rapid occupation of Denmark. This would mean that cruisers and destroyers would possibly not join in an action against the Danish Straits. The likeliest outcome is that some, if not all, of these ships would leave the Baltic and head for the Norwegian Sea before an armed conflict developed. That probability would become even higher should the number of corvette-type ships be increased.[14] If missile cruisers and missile destroyers were replaced by a large number of corvettes,

[14] The Soviet corvettes are small destroyers of approximately 800 tons. A distinction should be made between two differently armed types: the Nanuchka class has surface-to-surface missiles, and the Grisha class has AS torpedoes. The remaining armament is the same: surface-to-air missiles and 57-mm AA guns. The Nanuchka type proved unsatisfactory from a shipbuilding viewpoint and the series has been discontinued. A somewhat larger type with similar armament is now under construction and will have a 1,000-ton displacement.

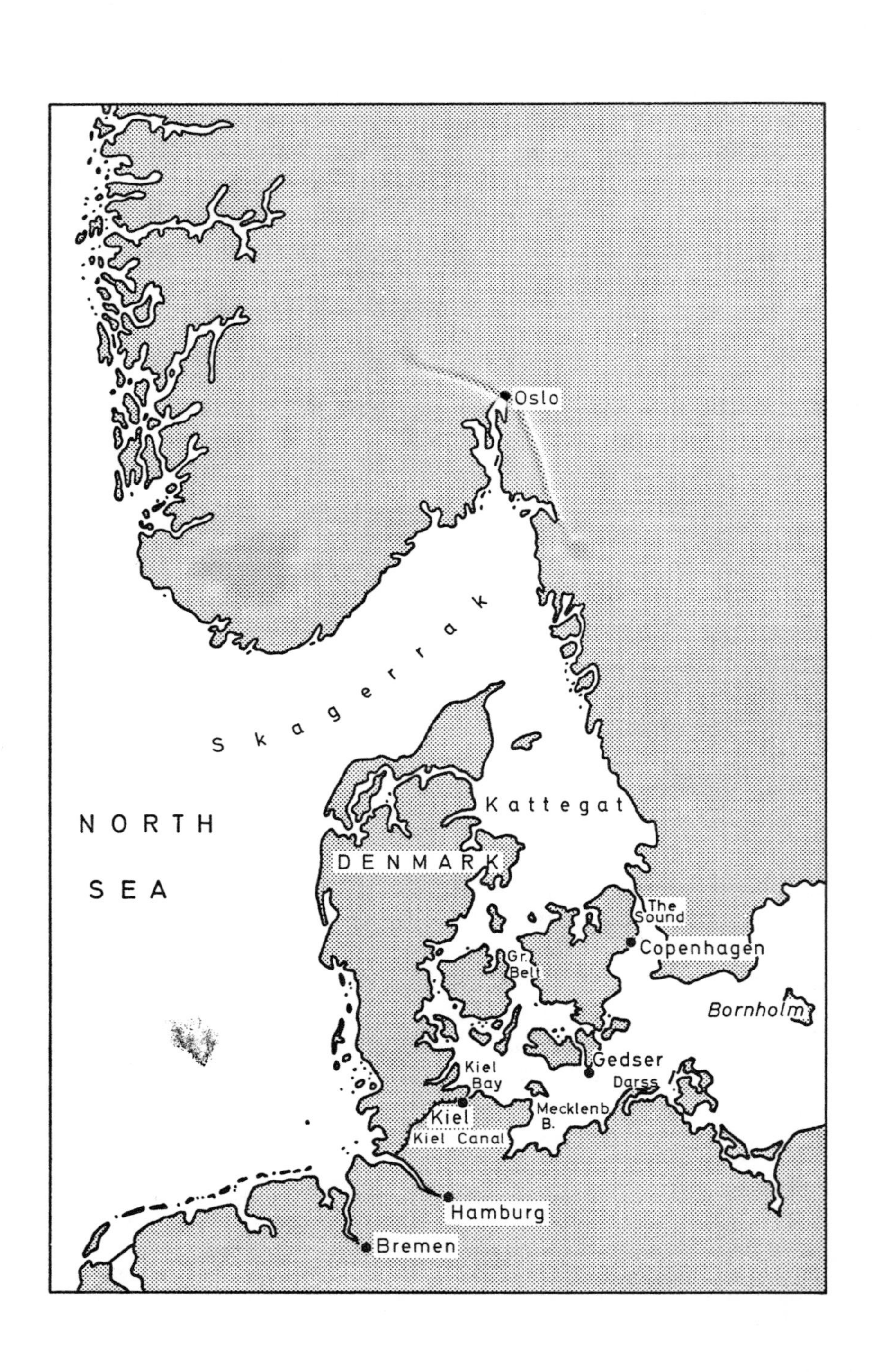

Oslo
Skagerrak
NORTH
SEA
Kattegat
DENMARK
The
Sound
Copenhagen
Gr.
Belt
Bornholm
Gedser
Kiel
Bay
Darss
Kiel
Mecklenb.
B.
Kiel Canal
Hamburg
Bremen

the fighting power of the Baltic Fleet would rather grow in relation to its special assignment.

The sea area between NATO coasts and Warsaw Pact coasts, being exceptionally narrow, weapon systems that elsewhere would be of low importance play a big role. This is particularly true of Soviet missile batteries along the coast. They can direct their missiles at targets at sea, but also at such stationary targets as harbor installations and airfields even farther away. The effect on land targets may be limited, if conventional warheads are used—their missiles are aerodynamic and cannot hit land targets with much precision—but if equipped with nuclear warheads, their missiles are dangerous weapons for which the West has no match.

Last, but not least, we should mention missile-equipped FPBs. In other sea areas they are used only in the immediate proximity of the coast. Since, in the Baltic, the coastal area and the overall theater of naval conflict coincide, these boats become a weapon not to be underestimated, provided of course that weather conditions are particularly advantageous. The navies of Poland and East Germany also possess such craft. On Darss, a narrow tongue of land between Rostock and Stralsund, an East German FPB base has been established and it permits very good surveillance of the Gedser narrows. After many years in which the Soviets maintained a monopoly of missile FPBs, the FPB flotilla of the Federal German Navy has finally moved in to offset that capability, at least partially.

NATO naval forces in the Baltic

Although the strategic objective of a Soviet attack in the Baltic can be unambiguously defined, operations in detail cannot, of course, be predicted. In principle, there are two alternatives: either, the aggressor would advance across the Elbe-Baltic Canal, occupy Schleswig-Holstein and Jutland via the land route, and attempt to attack the Danish islands from a westerly direction—in the course of these operations, the NATO front would have to incur the risk of landing operations seeking to outflank it; or, a direct attack would be made from the sea upon the Danish archipelago, especially the Zealand islands. A combination of the two operational possibilities is also conceivable. In either case, amphibious landings would be likely to play a decisive role in the struggle for the Baltic approaches. The principal mission of NATO naval forces in the Baltic, therefore, consists in countervailing such landing operations. One can hardly overstate the importance of this mission.

As a consequence of the key strategic role of the Baltic approaches, the Baltic mission is at the very center of the Federal German Navy's overall assignment. In this area, it provides the biggest contingent of NATO's defense forces. The Royal Danish Navy and the Royal Danish Air Force contribute valuable forces, but they are limited in numbers. More important than their numerical military contribution is the possibility that they provide for NATO naval and air forces to operate, in case of conflict, from the Danish area; as a general rule, advantageous geographic conditions provide a certain compensation to the West for the disadvantageous power ratio of approximately 1:6. NATO's naval forces in the Baltic are designed to make full use of these advantages. Fast patrol boats of various types, equipped with wire-guided torpedoes and antiship missiles, form their main component; then naval aviation, also equipped with antiship missiles, and small, conventionally propelled submarines of 430 tons displacement, particularly well suited for the Baltic.[15] Aircraft of the naval air squadrons in the Baltic have an exclusively combat mission, but no air defense mission. With respect to the FPBs, it is to be noted that they are substantially more seaworthy and faster than the missile-equipped FPBs of the East.

These advantages notwithstanding, NATO forces in the Baltic are sadly insufficient. The lack of land-based antiair missile batteries for the protection of harbors and airfields is an additional disadvantage. There are no antiship missile batteries. As it stands, NATO can only hope to employ delaying tactics and hold on until forces from outside arrive. But, except for expected support from carrier aircraft, further assistance can hardly be counted upon, if only because the Baltic theater today requires special types of ships which do not presently exist in the navies of those allies whose support could be hoped for. Assistance from American carrier aircraft has a special importance because

[15] These submarines stand good chances in the Baltic, even in the face of strong Soviet ASW capability. More than in other sea areas, the waters of the Baltic are stratified. The diversity of water layers may make the detection and localization of submarines difficult, if not impossible.

it would introduce tactical nuclear weapons. In the arsenal of both the Danish armed forces and the Federal German Navy there are no such weapons. An Eastern naval attack against the Danish narrows would push forward into an area that is free from nuclear weapons.

Finally one must add that the steady growth of naval armament on the Eastern side corresponds to a constantly dwindling budget for military investments in both Germany and Denmark. The balance of forces continues to slip. NATO finds itself compelled to make increasing use of mines as the defensive weapon *par excellence*. However, minelaying takes time. Here again, the time factor is of the essence for operations in the Baltic. If sufficient time were available for laying minefields systematically, then the defense mission could be more effectively fulfilled, although minefields will never provide absolute protection. For one thing, they can only take full effect if the adversary is prevented from conducting minesweeping operations.

No matter how one imagines an armed conflict in the Baltic to develop, one thing is certain: the West will never be the aggressor. The initiative is for the Soviet Union to take. There is a problem of decisive importance involved here with respect to timing, because no place is better suited for the unleashing of a sudden attack from one's present position than the sea. In view of the relatively short distance in the Baltic and of the high mobility of naval forces, an invader's fleet could at any moment show up off NATO coasts, be it in complete peace, be it in a period of crisis, be it in war. Such attack could be developed from maneuvers, or even without such pretext if troops had been embarked inconspicuously in more distant ports. Especially is Denmark threatened by the possibility of a surprise invasion supported by parachute troops, and possibly supplemented by the skillfully synchronized arrival of apparently harmless civilian cargo ships which in reality carry heavy military material.

Accordingly, NATO must brace itself for two different defense situations: for an attack which is known beforehand, and for a surprise *coup de main* attack that could not be counteracted in good time, or sufficiently, either for political reasons or simply because there was no prior warning. In the case of the first alternative, amphibious forces would have, at all costs, to be prevented from forging ahead, by minefields laid well in advance and by the use of all available forces. In the case of the second alternative, if indeed Warsaw Pact troops had already scored a *coup de main*, the task would be to close off the invasion area from any additional supplies coming in from the sea.

The North Sea

From the point of view of naval strategy, the Baltic and the North Sea form an entity. As long as Denmark and western and southern Norway remain in NATO hands, NATO possesses mastery of the sea in the North Sea by virtue of its superior position, even though its naval forces may be comparatively weak. Since Soviet shipping in the area would cease with the outbreak of war, the task of Western naval forces would be limited to safeguarding the approaches to the North Sea ports of Norway, Denmark, the Federal Republic of Germany, and of the east coast of England and Scotland. Although in the north Soviet surface ships and submarines have free access to the North Sea, the threat to these shipping routes is not very substantial. Seen from the naval theater in the Norwegian Sea, the North Sea, especially its southern part, forms a dead angle.

If, on the other hand, the positions of southern Norway, western Norway, and Denmark—all at once, or even only one of them—fell to the Soviets, the picture would, as already described, change completely. The Soviet Northern Fleet and the Baltic Fleet would establish themselves in full strength in these newly gained positions. Mastery of the sea would shift to the Soviets. NATO ports would be cut off from seaborne supplies. Shipping lanes along the English east coast and Britain's territory itself would be threatened.

NATO naval activity in the North Sea is therefore realistically conceivable only if Norway and Denmark continued to be controlled by NATO. The most important supply line would be the one leading through the southern North Sea to the main German estuaries. Since this runs through shallow water, the principal risk of former times—Soviet submarines—has become minor. Modern Soviet submarines are too big for these waters. Soviet surface ships are hardly a danger, in view of the distance from their base on the Kola Peninsula. The only real threat to NATO shipping stems from bomber aircraft flying in from the Baltic. They would attack either directly or indirectly via airborne minelaying.

Modern mines can be eliminated only at the price of

considerable minesweeping efforts. After they had been dropped by enemy aircraft, rerouting and losses would almost certainly be unavoidable. To protect against minelaying aircraft and against direct attacks upon shipping, a much higher number of missile-equipped ships would be required. The Federal German Navy has only three destroyers armed with antiair missiles: they are of the *Charles F. Adams* type.

In the central and northern North Sea, as well as in the Skagerrak and the eastern part of the Kattegat, water depths permit the deployment of bigger submarines. Here submarines are a greater threat than aircraft. German destroyers and escort vessels, as well as maritime patrol aircraft (MPA), have an obvious wartime mission in this respect.

It is an open issue whether Soviet missile cruisers and destroyers must also be expected to appear in the central North Sea and in the Skagerrak. As long as they have to start from the Kola base, their presence in these sea areas could only be for the purpose of making a brief raid. Yet, the very fact that Soviet naval operations in the immediate vicinity of the erstwhile world naval power of Great Britain can no longer be ruled out demonstrates fundamental changes in the naval strategic situation of the northern European area.

The simple conclusion is that NATO's defensive capability in the North Sea and in the Baltic is quite unsatisfactory. Yet, it may be said in closing that the significance of the Federal German and Danish navies for the power situation in this peripheral sea area can hardly be overstated. Their very existence counts. In order to appreciate their impact, one has only to imagine for a moment what the situation would be if they did not exist. The Baltic would be the domain of Moscow exclusively. The West would not be there. Denmark would be exposed to so great a military threat that its political attitude *vis-à-vis* NATO could hardly fail to be affected. Sweden would be more dependent upon Moscow, and even Finland would be drawn further into the Soviet sphere of power. The coasts of the Federal Republic of Germany, down to the westernmost recesses of the Baltic, would be indefensibly exposed to seizure by the Soviets. Defending Schleswig-Holstein on land, while the coast behind the front was not safeguarded, would be an illusory task. Thus one can only hope that the Federal German Navy, some present difficulties notwithstanding, will obtain, in the years to come, the means required for the fulfillment of its mission.

The Soviet Black Sea Fleet

The geographical situation in the Black Sea, despite some similarities, differs from that in the Baltic inasmuch as its NATO coast is the same length as its Soviet coast. But NATO does not exploit this advantage. There are no sufficiently equipped naval or naval air bases and, more important, no naval forces that can provide a match for the Soviet Black Sea Fleet.

In the Black Sea, again, we find the Soviet system of the "three waves": the coastal defense system contains the same elements as does that of the Baltic. The naval air arm is stationed in Crimea. The Crimean peninsula is centrally located and from it missile bombers can evenly and advantageously cover the entire Black Sea area. Thus Soviet coastal defense extends over the entire Black Sea.

Compared with this state of armament, the little Turkish Navy is of small weight only. Soviet naval power could be balanced only from outside. Nothing but a strong Western task force could hope to eliminate the Soviet Black Sea Fleet. However, just as in the Baltic, such a task force would have to incur an extremely high risk and face considerable losses. The entry of Western naval forces into the Black Sea in wartime must therefore be ruled out. This means that the Black Sea would be ceded to the Soviets. It has indeed become a Soviet domain. That being the case, the Black Sea Fleet discharges its defense mission simply by its existence and would therefore be available for offensive actions against the Anatolian coast, but primarily for supporting a land attack against the Dardanelles. A successful landing behind Turkish defense lines on either the European or the Asian flank of the Straits, would have the gravest consequences for their defense. In the case, conceivable after all, of the U.S.S.R. being unable to march through Rumanian and Bulgarian territory to attack the Straits, one can well imagine that an operation against them would be exclusively amphibious. Seizure of the Straits would alter fundamentally the naval strategic situation. The Black Sea Fleet would be able to abandon its defense mission and advance with all its forces—including units from coastal forces—to a new position at the Dardanelles. The Black Sea Fleet would become the Soviet Mediterranean Fleet and would be able to draw on the logistic potential of the Black Sea for Soviet naval warfare in the Mediterranean.

Under these circumstances, the Mediterranean would become the field of action of the Black Sea Fleet. We cannot, therefore, omit the Mediterranean from our analysis of the naval strategic situation in the European peripheral seas. Indeed, the Soviet high command is already emphasizing the *political* effects that result from stationing part of the Black Sea Fleet—the so-called Escadra—in the Mediterranean in peacetime. We shall return to these political effects in a later chapter dealing with the peacetime role of Soviet naval forces. At this point, it is enough to stress that most of these peacetime effects stem from the situation to be expected in an armed conflict. The question of who would win mastery of the sea in an eventual East-West naval war in the Mediterranean, especially the eastern Mediterranean, should therefore not only be answered on its own merits, but also has important implications for the peacetime presence of Soviet naval forces.

As in all analyses of naval strategy, the two factors of sea power, position and fleet, need examination. The naval strategic position of the West, primarily of the U.S. Sixth Fleet, is clear. It can rely on Turkish and Greek[15a] ports and, farther back, on Italian harbors and, hopefully, on Malta. The Soviets would start without any position whatsoever, and, having seized the Dardanelles—a prerequisite to any attempt at claiming mastery of the sea in the Mediterranean—their starting position would be in the innermost angle of the Aegean Sea, which offers few advantages and appears hardly satisfactory. There would be two possibilities for the Soviets to push ahead and broaden their Dardanelles position. They could, on the one hand, consider advancing through Bulgaria and the narrow strip of land that is the Greek province of Thrace with its harbor of Saloniki (and eventually proceed to occupy all of Greece); alternatively, they could utilize Yugoslavia's Adriatic coast, after having integrated Yugoslavia into the Soviet bloc, either politically—for instance, after the disappearance of Tito—or by occupation in direct or indirect

[15a]The changed situation of Greece within the NATO framework has not been considered here because the present study was completed prior to the Greek-Turkish dispute about Cyprus. But there is still a good reason for hope that Greece will return to full NATO membership, especially in case of a crisis or an armed East-West conflict.

connection with a war. The Adriatic is an interior sea with only one narrow access, the Strait of Otranto; hence, it is not ideally suited as a base for naval warfare in the Mediterranean. Nevertheless, broadening their geographical position from the Dardanelles to the Adriatic would provide the Soviets with an excellent factor of sea power if they were determined to wage the battle for mastery of the sea in the eastern Mediterranean. An increase of Soviet position along these lines would mean a corresponding loss of position for the West, which would then be limited to operating from the western access route to the eastern Mediterranean.

American aircraft carriers provide the hard core of Western naval forces in the Mediterranean. If necessary, they could eliminate the surface units of the Soviet Escadra, despite the strong antiair missile capability of the latter. On the other hand, in the relatively narrow Mediterranean the carriers themselves are seriously threatened. The risk of attacks from the air would be especially high—recent progress in the interception of bombers notwithstanding—if Soviet naval aviation from the Black Sea Fleet, possibly reinforced by squadrons from elsewhere, were able to start not only from Soviet or Greek bases, but also from Arab countries. A permanent or extended sojourn by aircraft carriers at a relatively small distance from Soviet bomber bases would entail a serious risk. In an air battle above the sea, carrier aircraft are at a disadvantage *vis-à-vis* land-based aircraft to the extent that the enemy's home base—the airfield on land—cannot be eliminated, at least not with conventional weapons, while the starting platform of one's own aviation could at any moment be sunk.

By its very nature, the aircraft carrier is an indispensable weapon for a fight on the ocean, i.e., in sea areas where land-based tactical air power cannot intervene. In peripheral seas that can be covered by land-based air power, the use of aircraft carriers in war is, in reality, no longer justified. Yet, the situation in the Mediterranean being what it is, Western mastery of that sea is inextricably linked to the continued presence and readiness of U.S. aircraft carriers. If they are already threatened from the air, they are even more seriously threatened by Soviet nuclear-powered submarines. We have already described the capability of such submarines to attack aircraft carriers in relatively narrow peripheral seas. Since the carriers are permanently stationed in the Mediterranean, they face the additional danger that Soviet nuclear submarines, noticed or unnoticed, could start tailing them even before a conflict developed, and attack immediately at X hour. Missile-equipped surface ships could likewise adopt that practice, although at a higher risk. In order to escape such surprise attack, which would herald the outbreak of war, the aircraft carriers might see fit to withdraw in the direction of the western Mediterranean, to reappear later, if possible with reinforcements. That would deprive the West of the advantages of their presence in the very first phase of conflict, when they would be needed to eliminate quickly the Escadra and to intervene in the fighting on land. If the carriers were withdrawn permanently, or for an extended length of time, or if the Soviets should succeed in eliminating them, cruisers and destroyers of the Black Sea Fleet with their superior ship-to-ship missiles, so far unmatched by the West, would carry the day.

It is easy to see that the situation of the U.S. Sixth Fleet in case of conflict would be a difficult one. Yet, it could be considerably improved. In the first place, NATO should respond to the Soviet challenge by redeploying part of its naval aviation and assigning it to land bases. A first step in this direction has been taken with the building of an air base on Crete.[15b] That island is particularly suited as a base because it serves as a door at the entrance to the Aegean Sea. In order to accomplish an impressive countermove to the extremely rapid gain of strength on the Soviet side, land-based naval aviation must, however, be increased and be more widely distributed. At the same time, more nuclear-powered submarines and ASW helicopter carriers should be assigned to the Sixth Fleet. Other NATO partners in the Mediterranean should do their share in controlling the submarine threat by making available ASW helicopters with seaborne and land bases.

These measures should enable NATO to maintain mastery of the sea in the eastern Mediterranean and, of course, in the western part of that sea. It is a fact, after all, that in a war situation, the West could concentrate the grand total of its naval forces in the Mediterranean, while the Soviets would only have *one* of their four fleets there, although they could concentrate their submarines and naval air arm.

If NATO manages to maintain its mastery of the sea, the sea routes for the support of Greece and Turkey will remain open. In

[15b]*See* Note 15a.

case of war, the Arab countries, including some of the oil-producing ones, would be separated from the center of Soviet power by a Western-dominated sea, and would finally be forced to side with the West. Oil could be freely transported to Europe by sea. Western mastery of the sea in the eastern Mediterranean would also cut sea links between the Soviet Black Sea Fleet and the Indian Ocean.

If, on the other hand, the West loses its mastery of the sea to the Soviets, everything would be dramatically different. Greece and Turkey would tumble. The southern flank of NATO would be ripped wide open. Middle Eastern oil, and indeed the entire Arab area, would fall into Soviet hands. The Suez Canal would open for the Soviets the passage to the Indian Ocean.

Soviet sea power in the Far East

In the Far East, the U.S.S.R. possesses a long-drawn-out coastline which borders, in part, on the open Pacific Ocean. Yet, in the case of war, the situation of the Soviet Far East Fleet would be no better than that of the other Soviet fleets. Not all its disadvantages stem from such natural causes as ice. Both Petropavlovsk, at the eastern tip of Kamchatka peninsula, and Vladivostok can be used year-round with the aid of ice-breakers, even though ice makes movement difficult during several months each year. The disadvantages are, again, of a geographical nature. Directly opposite the approach to Vladivostok, in the position of a barrier, lies the Japanese archipelago.

The approaches to the Sea of Japan—to the south, the Korea and Tsushima straits, to the north La Pérouse Strait—are easily controlled from Japanese territory. But even after passing those straits one has not reached the open seas. The Ryukyu Islands separate the East China Sea from the Pacific Ocean, and the Kuril Islands (these, to be sure, in Soviet possession) separate the Sea of Okhotsk from the Pacific Ocean. These island chains, too, constitute barriers to Soviet naval forces on their way to the ocean.

In establishing its base at Petropavlovsk, the U.S.S.R. tried to overcome its poor geographical endowment. Success was limited. The harbor is by now well equipped, but it has no road and railway links with the vast Siberian hinterland. In terms of naval strategy, it is almost an island. The sea connection between the geographically advanced base of Petropavlovsk and the central base of Vladivostok could not be safeguarded in war. The former would have to be supplied by surface ships and they would be exposed to considerable risk, particularly in the straits. Petropavlovsk may therefore play an important role primarily in submarine warfare, and especially in the first phase of a war. Yet, it is not a full-fledged naval strategic position. Soviet shipping cannot benefit from such a base.

As long as Japan does not have to be counted as a strong naval power in her own right, she provides a base for the U.S. fleet. Nowhere else does the Soviet Union find itself so directly confronted by American sea power. In the case of the Far East Fleet, therefore, the defense system of the "three waves"—as a defense scheme relating to an extended sea area off the coast—does not apply.

Soviet coastal defense would, it is true, be a threat to amphibious aggression. Naval aviation, defense submarines, and coastal forces safeguard the sea area immediately adjacent to the coast. Since, however, under present power conditions hardly anybody would aim at making a landing in eastern Siberia, these facts are not very significant.

The decisive fact is that the Soviet Far Eastern Fleet would find itself locked in the Sea of Japan as soon as war broke out. Even if there were not the difficulties of passing the straits, Soviet surface forces would not dare show themselves outside the Sea of Japan because of the U.S. Pacific Fleet. Even within that Sea, they would be in danger any time they ventured beyond the narrow range of coast-based air defenses. Even the possibility of a locally limited offensive in the Far East can safely be ruled out.

Vladivostok is the base for Soviet submarines in the Far East. Almost one-third of the total submarine fleet is stationed there. But for submarines, too, the geographical situation holds little promise. The narrow outlets that form the boundaries of the Sea of Japan, and, likewise, the small passages within the two island chains offer fine possibilities for the Americans to put their submarine-hunter submarines to use. The Soviets would have to reckon with the loss of submarines leaving on mission or returning to base. An additional handicap lies in the remoteness of the Soviet Far Eastern position: it is far removed from all the shipping routes in the Pacific that are vital to the West, except those leading to the Japanese islands. For Soviet submarines, this means long travel times to and fro, and consequently a reduction

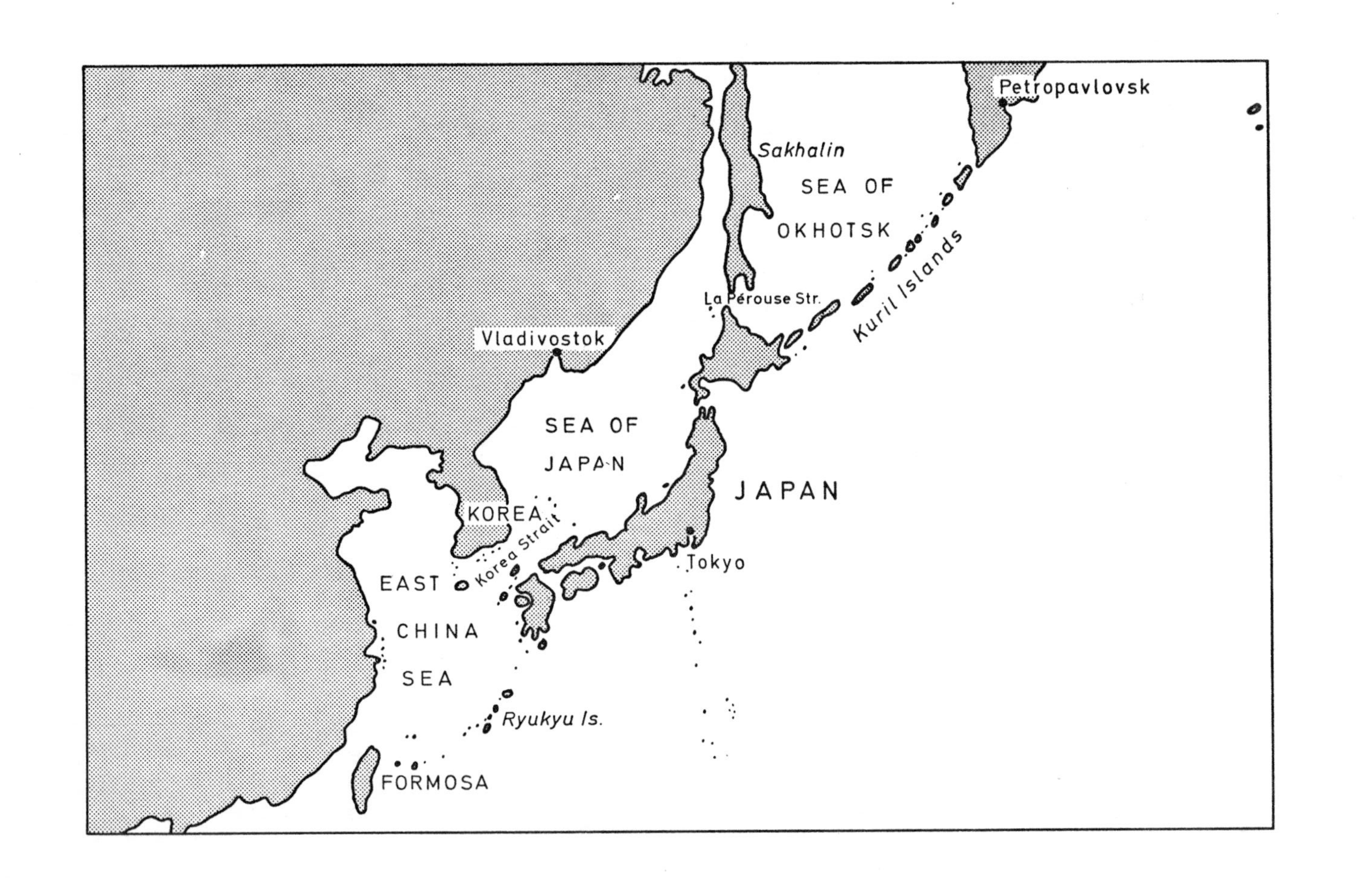
Petropavlovsk
Sakhalin
SEA OF
OKHOTSK
Kuril Islands
La Pérouse Str.
Vladivostok
SEA OF
JAPAN
JAPAN
KOREA
Korea Strait
Tokyo
EAST
CHINA
SEA
Ryukyu Is.
FORMOSA

of their potential. In spite of these drawbacks, the principal value of the Far Eastern Fleet in an East-West war would reside in its submarine forces.

In peacetime, the Far Eastern Fleet, together with the Black Sea Fleet, provides the reservoir that helps the U.S.S.R. to exercise its maritime presence in the Indian Ocean. But on the whole, and on the basis of the significance it would have for Soviet naval strategy in an East-West war, the Far Eastern Fleet has to be ranked behind the other three fleets. Its true strategic importance must be appreciated in a wider context, beyond the East-West conflict. First, there is the growing confrontation with China; then, there is the future of Japan as a country that is completely dependent on the sea. If Japan wants to protect its existence against the Soviet Union, it must, before anything else, acquire a naval capability that matches the Soviet Far Eastern Fleet.

As long as it lacks such naval potential, Japan is not independent in foreign policy. As long as there is the possibility of an East-West war, it must lean upon the country that has mastery of the sea, i.e., the United States. In case of war, Japan could opt for neither neutrality nor for the U.S.S.R. because its very existence depends on the lifelines at sea across the Pacific. And that is one thing the Soviets will never be able to offer. This state of affairs, on the other hand, enables the United States to count on the Japanese to make their inland seas, if not their territory, available in a war with the U.S.S.R.—no matter what Japanese policy might have been in the preceding period of peace.

A discussion of the role that the Soviet Far Eastern Fleet might play in relation to China is beyond the scope of this analysis which deals only with Moscow's offensive at sea against the West. Therefore, we can conclude this part of the analysis, which describes Soviet naval strategy in the sea areas adjacent to Soviet coasts. Condensed into a brief formula, the result can be stated as follows: *In all four naval districts, the Soviet Navy has fulfilled its defensive mission. In the three European districts it has moved on to a naval strategic offensive.*

4

the expansion of soviet naval strategy to the oceans

Sea power on the oceans

Until a few years ago, Soviet leaders appeared audacious when they publicly boasted of being on a par with the West on the oceans, too. Neither the presence of Soviet submarines practicing "raider warfare," nor the stationing of strategic atomic submarines in ocean areas justified Admiral Gorshkov's claim when he said: "Sooner or later the USA must learn to understand that they have ceased to rule the oceans," a statement that was not by any means in keeping with naval strategic conditions as they then were. Yet, the "sooner or later" clearly demonstrated the objective.

It is extremely difficult for the U.S.S.R. to get closer to the realization of its objective of ruling the oceans, because any attempt to deny the United States mastery of the oceans in wartime and to replace it with Soviet mastery of the sea requires the establishment of sea power on the oceans. This again has two prerequisites: first, the construction of an "adequate fleet," i.e., naval means that would be suitable, in quantity and quality, for eliminating the naval forces that make for Western sea power; and secondly, a naval strategic position from which this process of elimination could be carried on, that would allow the subsequent establishment of Soviet sea power, and that could become the point of origin of the Soviet Union's own shipping.

Both prerequisites are now lacking. The Soviet Union has so far been unable to match the big U.S. aircraft carriers on which Western mastery of the oceans still rests. Soviet naval strategic positions are a long way from the oceans. Even the position on the Norwegian Sea, which is fairly advantageously situated in relation to the ocean, is, as was pointed out earlier, separated from the ocean by the Scotland-Iceland gap. Surface ships passing through could not avoid detection,[16] and would be attacked by land-based naval aviation as well as by Western submarines.

The only military arm that the Soviets could disptach from their remote positions to the oceans without incurring such dangers is their submarine fleet. However, in spite of certain technical improvements, the conventional submarine remains what it was at the end of the Second World War, a useful instrument for sinking cargo vessels, but an instrument unsuitable for a systematic fight against an enemy's "fleet." Compelled by air surveillance to cruise almost all the time under water, it lacks operational speed and is insufficiently equipped for attacking destroyer-escorted aircraft carriers.

By virtue of these facts, for decades the Soviets had no alternative on the oceans to a strategy of "raider warfare" by submarines. This method is, as may be remembered, a weaker form of naval warfare, and since in adopting it, one renounces the struggle for mastery of the sea, it is at the same time indicative of a naval strategic defensive. It consists of circumventing the enemy's sea power and attempting to seize directly the object of naval warfare, i.e., the cargo vessel. By embracing a "raider warfare" strategy, the Soviets would leave the oceans and the control of oceanic shipping lanes to the West. In wartime, they would have to forego their own shipping on the oceans, as well as the exercise of power in overseas areas subject to their influence. Not even the most brilliant successes of their submarines or the most painful loss of tonnage to the West would, in principle, change that state of affairs. At the outbreak of war, the Soviet flag would disappear from the world's oceans. This would

[16] The situation would not change materially in the unlikely event that the U.S. naval air base at Keflavik, Iceland, became unavailable in a conflict, since the Americans would still have their base on Greenland. Faced with the prospect of Soviet invasion, Iceland, a member of NATO, would in the last analysis prefer the protection that NATO provides.

be true of commercial shipping, but just the same would hold for all surface ships of the Soviet Navy.

As long as the United States had to reckon only with Soviet raider warfare, their mastery of the oceans was undisputed. Certainly, the safety of its shipping was a matter of concern to the United States, but Soviet ambitions aiming at oceanic sea power could be easily discounted as illusory. As long as the U.S.S.R. did not build aircraft carriers, the Americans did not perceive any danger to their own mastery of the oceans.

Today, we can no longer accept without question such an idyllic tableau, so entirely favorable to the West. We must inquire whether the Soviets have not after all acquired the ability to question Western mastery of the oceans, even from their ill-suited position. If they built aircraft carriers or devised other technical means, could they change the naval strategic situation on the oceans, just as they did in the peripheral seas? As we have seen, Soviet fleets now consist of three elements: missile bombers, missile-equipped surface ships, and submarines. Could the Soviets today use these instruments to eliminate American aircraft carriers, the foundation of Western mastery of the sea? To analyze the question, the emphasis must be on the word *today*. Future possibilities, especially those implied in the build-up of a Soviet aircraft carrier fleet, will be discussed at a later point.

How to attack aircraft carriers on the oceans

The situation as regards possible bomber attacks upon American aircraft carriers is clear: the Soviets have no missile-equipped aircraft with sufficient operational radius to reach them. The four-engine, long-distance aircraft that they use in peacetime maneuvers for reconnaissance missions above the ocean are not suitable for attack operations because of their armament and small numbers. Furthermore, they are relatively slow. Given the speed of Western hunter aircraft, they could not even be used for reconnaissance in a wartime situation, unless they were protected by hunter aircraft of their own.

As regards missile cruisers and missile destroyers, it is frequently said in the relevant literature that they are not only well suited for use on the oceans, but they were primarily designed and earmarked by the Soviets for such use. The present author finds himself unable to concur. Even if these ships took the risk of passing through the narrows—in the case of the Northern Fleet through the Scotland-Iceland-Greenland gap—soon after attaining the ocean they would be compelled to replenish their fuel supply, since their operational radius is quite limited. Present possibilities of radar surveillance by air have made the former practice of inconspicuously stationing tankers in remote sea areas beforehand little more than a memory. A task force of Soviet missile ships out on an oceanic mission would, therefore, have to take along its own tankers in order to ensure its safety, especially from air attacks. Thus the operational speed of the missile cruiser/destroyer task force would be slowed down to tanker speed. For this reason alone oceanic missions seem to be ruled out, and the argument that the Soviets designed these ships primarily for assignments in ocean areas can hardly stand in the face of these technical facts. Had they considered assignments in ocean areas, the Soviets would have designed the ships for greater cruising radius in the first place.

If one examines the operational possibilities for missile ships in an ocean environment, one can safely assume (as we already did when studying conditions in the peripheral seas) that carrier-based aircraft would have some success in attacking surface ships strongly protected by antiair missiles, albeit at the price of considerable losses. American nuclear-powered submarines could also be used against Soviet task forces, and would be likely to score. Damage done to one or several ships would put the commander of the task force in a difficult position, if he was operating in an area where the enemy possessed mastery of the sea and there was no naval strategic position in easy reach. The Soviet admiral would not be able to risk sending damaged ships home by themselves, because especially as they passed through the narrows, they would be easy prey for Western aircraft and nuclear-powered submarines. Damaged ships would, therefore, compel the task force commander either to divide his force in two, or to cancel the operation altogether.

Let us still assume that the Soviets overcame these handicaps: what would be the chances of Soviet surface vessels being able to hit U.S. carriers with their long-range ship-to-ship missiles? Obviously, it would not be possible to approach to within visual sighting or radar-contact range before firing on the carrier. Firing the missile from farther away, however, would require the prior establishment of a chain of reconnaissance aircraft relaying information as to the carrier's position. It is doubtful that this would be feasible in the presence of carrier-based aircraft. Since the operational radii of carrier aircraft by far exceed the firing range of Soviet missiles, the carriers would be able at any time to attack the Soviet ships, while easily evading any approach to them that might carry a risk: their information on the relative positions would be complete owing to their reconnaissance aircraft, and the speed of the Soviet force would be limited by its accompanying fuel-supply ships. Soviet missile ships would have no tactical chance to hit the carriers with their missiles, indeed they would not be able even to get into firing position.[17]

The conclusion is that the task of destroying American aircraft carriers in the open seas by means of ship-to-ship missiles is impossible. Yet, as long as the carriers are at sea and ready for action, there is no other useful task for Soviet surface ships to perform on the ocean. An oceanic operation conducted away from a naval strategic position that can at any time safely be resorted to, is an operation in an area controlled by the enemy, where the ratio between chance and risk becomes extremely unfavorable. The Soviet high command would hardly be willing to risk premature attrition of its fleet in the course of such operations. It is more likely to save for later whatever of its forces are not needed for warfare in the peripheral seas. A need for missions in the oceans might well arise in a later phase, but only after the American aircraft carriers had been eliminated by other means.

The Soviet submarine fleet

If bomber aircraft and surface vessels are not the appropriate means with which to engage in the battle for mastery of the oceans against the West, there is the third and, indeed, the most important element of Soviet naval armament: the submarine fleet. In order to find out whether the picture is changing in this respect, it is necessary to review in more detail the present state of Soviet submarine development.

With its approximately 400 boats, the Soviet submarine fleet

[17] The fact that the more recent series of Soviet missile destroyers and cruisers are armed with antiship missiles of a lesser range than previous models seems to indicate that the Soviets are getting away from long shots which can be targeted only with the assistance of a chain of several aircraft relays.

is the biggest such fleet that has ever existed in peacetime. It is frequently compared with the German submarine fleets of the two world wars. The conclusion is then often drawn that Western shipping, which was extremely endangered by a far less numerous German submarine fleet, would be in an all-but-hopeless position in a future war, given the enormous number of Soviet vessels. Conclusions of this nature grossly oversimplify the problem. For, in sharp contrast to the German submarine fleet which was geared exclusively towards raider warfare, the present Soviet submarine fleet is not by any means so single-purpose. It has other important missions to perform.

Strategic atomic submarines

Availability for strategic atomic war has first priority among the missions assigned to the Soviet submarine fleet. As shown above, submarines designed and constructed for this mission cannot make a contribution to naval warfare. Accordingly, they constitute a special contingent within the Soviet submarine fleet. Within that contingent, there is a—decreasing—number of older types, some with conventional propulsion, some with nuclear propulsion, some equipped with cruise missiles, some with ballistic missiles. They were not specifically designed for their atomic mission, but are converted attack submarines. As a consequence, they cannot carry more than three or four strategic atomic missiles on each assignment. Their gravest handicap is the short range of their missiles. Depending on the location of their targets, they would have to approach very close to the U.S. coast, where they could be detected and localized by a sonar receiver network laid out and wired on the bottom of the sea. Hence, their contribution to the atomic strike potential is of questionable value. These submarines were commissioned as a makeshift response to American Polaris submarines. Not until ten years later, in 1967, were the Soviets able to come up with a new type more or less equivalent to the Polaris submarine. These new submarines, whose NATO code name is Yankee class, will gradually replace the former makeshift variety.

As do the American submarines which they emulate, the Yankee submarines carry sixteen missiles, whose range corresponds to that of the original Polaris missiles. Although their displacement is higher, they are quite a bit slower than the

Polaris submarines. Their rate of construction has been greatly accelerated. The total number of Yankee submarines commissioned and under construction in 1973 is estimated at 33.[18] In the meantime, the Americans have continued to equip their strategic atomic submarines with missiles of an ever-increasing range. The most recent missile models—Polaris A-3 and Poseidon—attain almost 5,000 km. The Soviets soon matched and have even exceeded this rapid progress. Their latest ballistic submarine missiles can attain a range of almost 7,000 km, if their explosive charge is sufficiently lowered. Since these missiles are heavier and longer than their predecessors, the submarines have undergone some redesigning and can carry only 12 of them. The Yankee submarines that carry 12 missiles constitute a new class, for which the NATO code name Delta class has been introduced. Some of them have been commissioned, while others are under construction. The assumption that the Soviets would shortly come up with a new type designed to carry the original larger number of missiles—possibly with a missile featuring further improvements—has recently been proved correct.

Since completion of their program to construct Polaris-type boats, the Americans have not undertaken any more submarine construction, but have limited themselves to improving their ballistic missiles. Apart from increasing the range of their missiles, they have concentrated on improving the quality of the warheads. Polaris A-3 and Poseidon missiles are or will be equipped with Multiple Independently Targeted Reentry Vehicle (MIRV) warheads. If MIRV warheads are used, it will be possible to multiply the number of targets assigned to the missile. When the negotiations for SALT I were concluded, the Soviets did not possess MIRV technology.

Relying on the MIRV monopoly they then had, the Americans settled for a limit of 44 strategic atomic submarines with a total of 710 missiles, while the Soviets were allowed 62 submarines with 950 missiles.[18a] The Soviets thus obtained from the SALT negotiations a considerable numerical superiority in submarines and missiles, not to mention the fact that every single one of their missiles is also superior in megatonnage. In addition,

[18] According to *Jane's Fighting Ships*, 1974/75.

[18a] It may well be that these figures will lose their relevance if a SALT II agreement based on the recent Ford-Brezhnev talks should be reached.

they enjoy at least a temporary advantage with respect to the range of their Delta missiles. It has taken the Soviets surprisingly little time to acquire MIRV technology and, as soon as they apply it to their submarine ballistic missiles, they will have, on balance, absolute superiority in their sea-based atomic strike potential.

Attack submarines for antiship operations

The number of submarines that the Soviets have available for naval warfare proper, i.e., the sum total minus the special group of strategic atomic units, runs far over 300. Presently, it is true, the large majority is still conventionally propelled. Nuclear-powered submarines have a share of approximately 17 percent, and as yet only a few of these are of a truly advanced design. The remainder hail from the period when the Soviets were still in the process of developing nuclear-powered submarines, and are relatively slow and particularly noisy.

Not all the submarine fleet, even as it is here described, is available for oceanic warfare. One must first subtract the submarines needed for defensive tasks in the four Soviet naval districts. If all defense positions are continuously manned, the number of units required for this task is considerable. This assignment is given by preference to submarines of a medium operational radius, not suited for use on the oceans, or less economical elsewhere, i.e., older submarines with conventional propulsion. Soviet maneuvers prove, however, that nuclear-powered submarines, especially those equipped with antiship missiles, are also assigned to these tasks. Without them, the "second wave" of the Soviet long-range naval defense system would lose in effectiveness. The number of submarines left for use in ocean areas is distributed in the proportion of two-thirds for the Atlantic and one-third for the Pacific.

For the extended deployment of submarines on the oceans, the old rule of thumb is still valid today: one-third at the home base for outfitting and maintenance, one-third engaged in traveling to and fro, and the remaining third on mission. For nuclear-powered submarines the percentage actually spent on mission may be higher. In principle, however, the rule of thumb still holds true. The determining factor for the length of time submarines remain in their areas of operation is not the fuel supply but is, in most cases, the stock of ammunition. If one calculates on this basis the average number of submarines stationed on the oceans at any given time, one obtains approximately 45 submarines, of which 18 are nuclear-powered, for the northern and southern Atlantic. From this figure we must subtract the submarines required for the Mediterranean and those needed for special tasks, e.g., around the Cape of Good Hope and in the Indian Ocean. Especially for the Mediterranean a considerable number of nuclear-powered units should be assumed. One may presume that half that number of submarines are on station simultaneously in the Pacific. Obviously, these rough calculations are based on a certain number of assumptions and cannot be mathematically precise. Still, they provide some indications for an evaluation of the current submarine threat on the oceans.

These figures are averages for an assumed prolonged war. They must not lead us to underestimate the threat presented by Soviet submarines. The Soviets could, for instance, dispatch all their combat-ready submarines simultaneously to the area of operations at the very beginning of an armed conflict. They would then deliberately accept that the number of submarines later to be engaged in the regular rotation sequence would decrease. However, as conventional submarines are increasingly replaced by nuclear-powered units, the number of submarines to be retained for the "second wave" of the Soviet defense set-up could be reduced, because of the greater effectiveness of nuclear submarines. This would, again, raise the number of units available for deployment on the oceans. With nuclear-powered submarines one does not have to differentiate between large and medium operational radii. This fact provides flexibility and permits the center of gravity of operations to be quickly shifted, as circumstances dictate, from the peripheral seas to the oceans and vice versa.

Submarine-hunting with attack submarines

The preceding section dealt with submarine operations against surface ships. In modern naval warfare submarines have acquired an additional mission: fighting other submarines. As regards submarines that are armed only with torpedoes, one no longer distinguishes between attack submarines and hunter/killer submarines. Such submarines are equally suited for use against surface ships and for submarine-hunting. The differences do not lie in the technical equipment, but in the assignment and, perhaps, in the variety of torpedoes that they take along on their missions.

Underwater submarine-hunting can be carried on in two ways: either by waiting for enemy submarines that might approach—outside harbors, or close to narrows where they must pass, or by pursuing an enemy submarine that has been detected and localized. For the former, one can use conventional submarines. For the latter, superior speed on the part of the pursuing submarine is a prerequisite; hence, only nuclear-powered units qualify. In a submarine-against-submarine struggle, a low noise level and the quality of acoustic equipment are of obvious significance. He who can detect and localize the enemy while remaining unnoticed himself will be the winner of the underwater duel. Thus, a submarine-against-submarine fight is, at the same time, a competition between the sensoring devices on either side.

The possibility of destroying submarines by submarines takes on overriding importance where strategic atomic submarines are concerned. Yet, a systematic search for enemy submarines by submarines of one's own is evidently pointless in the vastness of ocean areas, because the size and depth of the oceans defy such an undertaking. One can hope to detect and localize a strategic atomic submarine only when it leaves its base or passes through a strait. But then it is sufficient to register its noise. Noise spreads much farther below the water surface than in the air space above the water. If its speed is superior, a hunter/killer submarine can attach itself to, and pursue, a submarine simply by following the source of noise. The hunter submarine cannot be shaken off and may continue its pursuit to the assigned station of the victim, "shadow" it there, and then destroy it at the very moment of the outbreak of war or, at latest, after the victim has fired its first missile. Sea-based atomic potential could thus lose its invulnerability and, hence, its deterrent effect. Deterrence would become questionable.

In the beginning, U.S. Polaris submarines had greater speed than their Soviet counterparts; accordingly, the Soviets were not able to constitute a threat for the Polaris submarines. All they could do was lie in wait outside U.S. bases, register the passage of Polaris submarines, and identify their specific noise—their so-

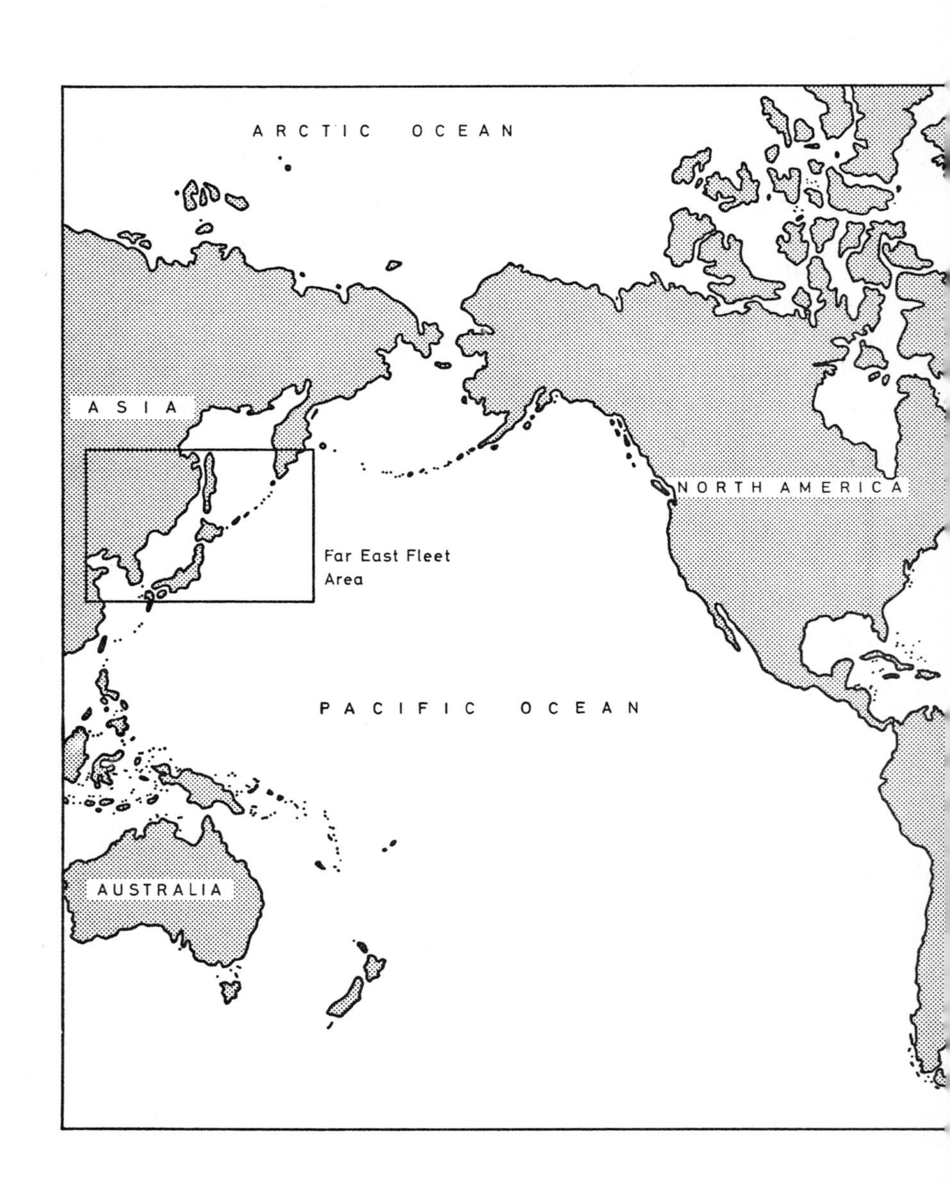
ARCTIC OCEAN
ASIA
NORTH AMERICA
Far East Fleet
Area
PACIFIC OCEAN
AUSTRALIA

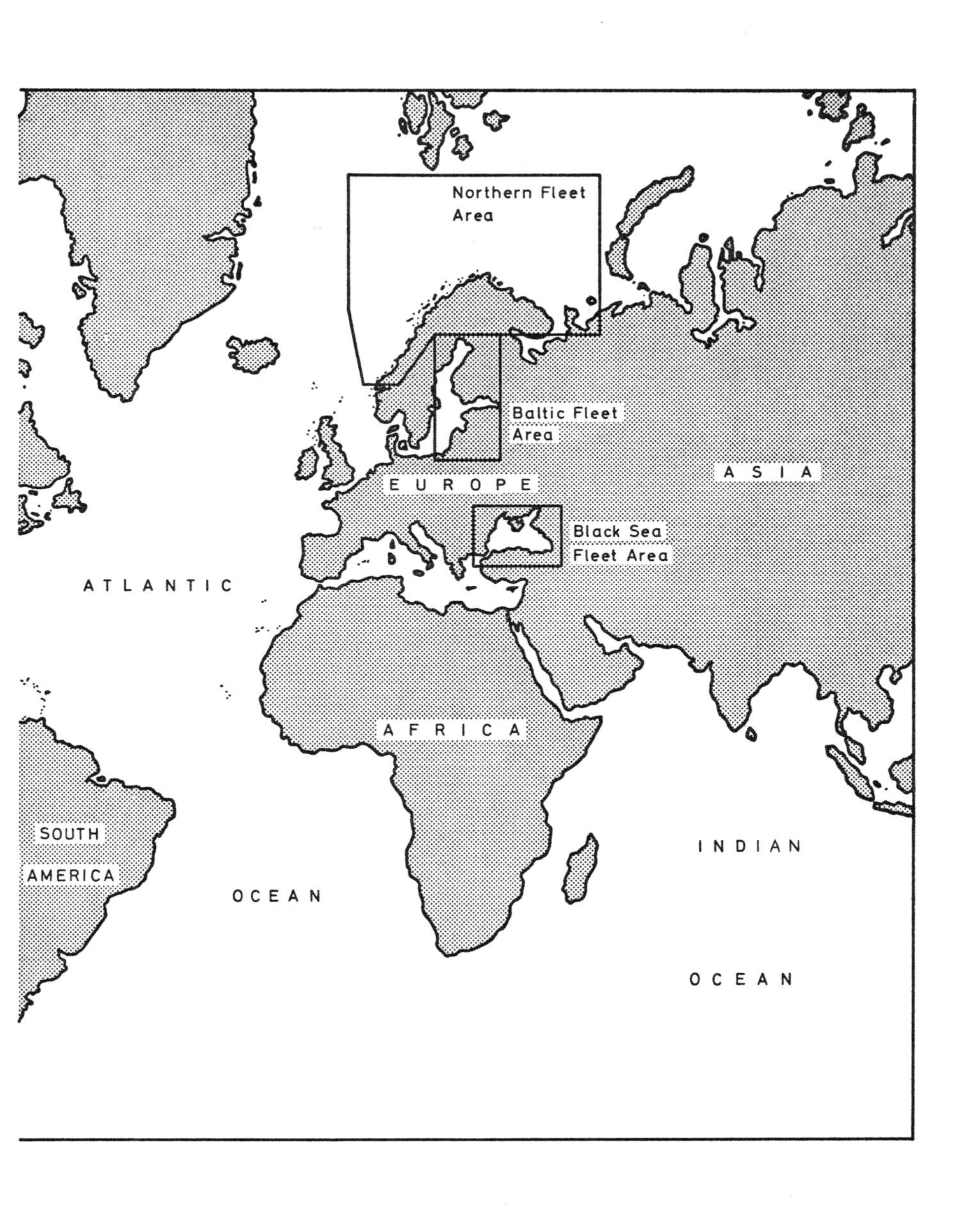
Northern Fleet Area
Baltic Fleet Area
EUROPE
ASIA
Black Sea Fleet Area
ATLANTIC
AFRICA
SOUTH AMERICA
OCEAN
INDIAN
OCEAN

called signature, in itself a valuable piece of information. They could not pursue them to their firing positions. Now, the Soviets have attack submarines, if as yet in limited numbers, that are superior in speed at least to the older series of Polaris submarines and can be used to tail Polaris submarines. In spite of these recent Soviet achievements, the sea-based atomic potential of the United States cannot, as yet, be considered seriously threatened.

Given their faster attack submarines, the Americans have developed a similar capability and are no less effective. As long as Soviet strategic atomic submarines had to be stationed close to the U.S. coast, it was not necessary even to shadow them: they were exposed to American ASW measures anway. With the introduction of their Yankee and Delta submarines, which are stationed far off the coast, the Soviets have successfully overcome that threat, and, with respect to the strategic atomic issue, made inroads on U.S. mastery of the oceans. Nevertheless, they have not attained invulnerability. There is no way for them to avoid having their sea-based atomic potential tailed and shadowed by Western nuclear-powered hunter/killer submarines.[19]

On the other hand, nuclear-powered hunter/killer submarines are still a rare commodity on the American side, too. Neither side

[19] In areas where another power possesses mastery of the sea, strategic atomic submarines are exposed to stationary ASW from the surface, although chances of detection are slight. One would therefore prefer to station one's strategic atomic submarines outside the adversary's area of control and, if possible, within one's own realm of mastery of the sea. This provides the motive for maximizing the range of missiles carried by strategic atomic submarines.

In this context, it might well be that the Soviets, considering the range of their Delta-class missiles, envisage covering targets in the United States across the North Pole from waters close to their Arctic Ocean position, i.e., from the Barents Sea and possibly also from sea areas east of Novaya Zemlya. By stationing strategic atomic submarines in these areas, they could avoid venturing through the dangerous narrows into the Atlantic. They could also work out plans to equip these limited, shallow seas under their control with networks of sonar cables, which would enable them to localize any Western hunter/killer submarine. In view of the Soviets' strong ASW capability in this northern position, any Western attempt to shadow and tail their strategic atomic submarines would be futile. Western hunter/killer submarines would risk being eliminated before they could hope to eliminate their potential Soviet victims. These scenarios are, of course, highly speculative. At present, there are no indications that the Soviets are planning in this direction. Also, tactical countermeasures to deprive such Soviet schemes of their effect could be devised.

is presently able to completely shadow the sea-based atomic potential of the other. Let us remember that only a few Soviet nuclear submarines of advanced design and superior speed face 41 U.S. submarines of the Polaris type, not counting the strategic atomic submarines of Great Britain and France. Once both sides possess substantial numbers of nuclear-powered attack submarines suited for submarine-hunting, it could very well be that a majority of them will have to be earmarked for submarine-hunting assignments. They would thus not be available for other missions. This holds true for both sides. In particular it would proportionately reduce the number of Soviet submarines that, as calculation above has shown, could be stationed on the oceans.

The Trident submarine

Although everything essential to an assessment of the Soviet submarine fleet has already been said, it appears useful—because of the close links with the general problem of submarine-hunting by submarine—to insert a section on recent American developments in the field of strategic atomic submarines. In view of the high priority that the Americans must assign to the invulnerability of their sea-based atomic potential, they are forced to react to the growing numbers of ever-faster Soviet nuclear hunter submarines. Some measure against the increasing threat to their strategic atomic submarines must be found. The best response, of course, would be superior speed of the strategic atomic submarine itself, which would allow it to shake off its followers.

This is, unfortunately, not feasible. Designed to carry a heavy load, the strategic atomic submarine will always lose the race against a small hunter/killer submarine, which is specially designed for high-speed performance. If, then, speed does not offer a solution, one must try to make it difficult for the hunter submarine to establish "contact" with its potential victim. As pointed out, the critical area for detection is the one adjacent to one's own base, through which the strategic atomic submarine must pass after each stay at its home base, in order to reach its assigned position. In a war situation, one would certainly try to keep this area free of enemy submarines by massive employment of ASW forces. But what counts is the shadowing and tailing of strategic atomic submarines *before* the outbreak of war, or rather as a peacetime activity generally. But under the conditions prevailing in peacetime one cannot prevent the enemy's hunter submarines from sojourning in the sea area near one's own bases.

The solution may well lie in the construction of strategic atomic submarines that feature four essential qualities: extremely low noise level, ultra-high missile-firing range, deep-diving capability, and ability to stay at sea for an almost unlimited time. The Americans are presently building a strategic atomic submarine that will meet these requirements: the Trident submarine. The first boat is planned to be ready for use in 1978. The first version of the Trident missile is to attain more than 10,000 km. With this range, the target area which could be covered would increase twentyfold. Accordingly, the sea area from which all strategic targets in the Soviet power sphere could be reached would grow enormously. The northern and southern Atlantic, as well as the Pacific and the Indian Ocean, would become potential areas for stationing. To begin with, priority seems to be assigned to the Pacific. A base to cater to Trident submarines is planned for Puget Sound, in the vicinity of Seattle.

In the construction of the Trident submarines, particular emphasis is to be placed upon the reliability of all systems, in order to minimize the necessity of returning to base. Rotation of crew, replenishment, and possibly even resupply of missiles, are to take place somewhere on the high seas. If a Trident should, on occasion, be forced to return to its base, then its low noise level on departure would make its detection difficult. Should a Trident submarine be detected and localized, it would dive below a very deep specific layer of water that is present throughout the oceans, is impervious to sound, and would therefore absorb the remaining low level of noise; the pursuer would lose track. Given the present state of the art, the atomic potential placed upon Trident submarines can thus be considered truly invulnerable.

With the construction of the Trident submarine, the United States will once more have an advantage over its adversaries in the field of strategic atomic submarines. The sea-based atomic potential of the Soviets, by contrast, is largely linked, and will remain linked for some time, to the Yankee/Delta submarines which are presently under construction or about to be introduced. These submarines are ineluctably exposed to the threat of highly advanced American hunter/killer submarines, and hence permanently vulnerable.

Anti-carrier operations by submarines

Let us return to the question of what the Soviets can do against Western mastery of the sea. Are they today in a position to threaten it by massive use of their submarines against U.S. aircraft carriers? Between the two world wars, one took it for granted that the Germans could primarily use their submarines on the oceans to disturb Allied shipping, i.e., as an instrument of raider warfare. In the decades since the end of World War II, the same assumption was made about the Soviets. Systematic operations by conventionally propelled submarines against fast, mobile forces in the vast spaces of the ocean were out of the question. All prerequisites were lacking: there was no large-scale reconnaissance in sea areas, and submarines had neither the operational speed to approach reported ship targets over major distances, nor the tactical speed needed to attack strongly escorted aircraft carrier task forces. Submarine attacks were limited to chance encounters where conditions happened to be favorable.

It is different with nuclear-powered submarines. They have the necessary operational and tactical speeds. Modern submarines with their advanced acoustic equipment are also able to localize surface ships at a distance far exceeding the range of visual perception. Yet, for orderly operational planning, they require reconnaissance data. A full-fledged submarine war against U.S. aircraft carriers would, then, presuppose the fulfillment of two conditions: first, the availability of a sufficient number of high-speed, nuclear-powered submarines; secondly, the possession of data from large-scale, continuous reconnaissance.

We cannot judge the extent to which the Soviets would have information on the ocean areas in case of conflict. Since they do not have a sufficient number of fast naval reconnaissance aircraft with the necessary operational radius, they would have to rely on satellite information. We will return to this aspect in a later context.

In view of the steadily growing number of Soviet nuclear-powered attack submarines, and on the assumption that the Soviets do, in fact, have a fully working satellite reconnaissance system, new possibilities for systematic submarine operations against aircraft carriers could indeed open up. In the West, strategic planners expect a new Soviet submarine strategy which would presumably have two phases. As part of Phase I, even before the outbreak of war, they would dispatch to the oceans all their available long-range submarines, in order to effect a concentrated, centrally directed operation against U.S. aircraft carriers. This action would take precedence over any raider warfare activities. Nuclear-powered submarines would form the core of the submarine force. Conventional submarines would be positioned in an echelon formation of considerable width and depth along the routes of probable forward movement of the carriers. They would attack in case of chance encounters, but otherwise they would provide reconnaissance for the nuclear submarines. Only after the carriers had been destroyed or the operation had failed due to insufficient reconnaissance, would the Soviets proceed to Phase II. They would then move on to raider warfare.

How would one evaluate the prospects of a submarine strategy of this nature? As regards the degree of concentration, we have already concluded that the Soviet submarine fleet still consists primarily of conventional submarines. The number of nuclear-powered submarines available for ocean warfare is limited, and there are not yet many units of advanced design. That would hold true even if the Soviets, at the beginning of a war, were to throw in all their nuclear-powered submarines at the same time (with the exception of those engaged in hunting strategic atomic submarines), regardless of any reasonable rhythm of rotation. It is still quite doubtful whether under present circumstances enough submarines would be available to cover the vast ocean areas that an anti-carrier operation of this nature would have to include. An additional handicap would be speed: the majority of today's Soviet nuclear-powered submarines run only between 20 and 30 knots, depending on construction date. Catching up with rapidly advancing carrier task forces is a mission they could tackle only from a forward position.

One conceivable stratagem would be to position nuclear-powered submarines in the immediate vicinity of individual aircraft carriers even before the outbreak of hostilities. In the section on the Mediterranean, we referred to that possibility. If such positioning were successful, the submarine could attack the carrier at the very moment when war began, or, Pearl Harbor style, even before, thereby deliberately starting war. This presupposes, of course, that the submarine could remain unnoticed. Otherwise, the carrier could take off at top speed and possibly shake off the submarine, depending on relative speeds. Even if it remained unnoticed, a submarine that was slower than the shadowed carrier could not bear with its potential victim for any length of time, again for reasons of speed. Looking at the overall situation, one can conclude that the possibility of rapidly eliminating the bigger part of the U.S. carrier fleet does not as yet exist.

What Soviet submarine strategy could possibly achieve today is damage to or destruction of individual carriers. Besides, the arrival of carriers in Western Europe could very well be delayed by such actions, and there could be a corresponding delay in support for the war in the Norwegian Sea and in the Baltic. That would be an accomplishment for the Soviet side. Otherwise, Soviet strategy as here described appears, at most, as a prefiguration of a future when the number of nuclear-powered submarines has increased considerably and their speed has been improved.

Raider warfare by submarines

Whatever chance of success this strategy might harbor, the Soviets would not incur much of a risk by adopting it. They could at any moment switch over to Phase II, i.e., raider warfare. Shortly after the beginning of a war, before convoy services had been organized and before Western antisubmarine air surveillance was in full swing, the presence of all their available submarines at sea might bear fruit.

If the Soviets continued raider warfare for an appreciable period of time, the situation concerning oversea transport could become critical for the West. Because of the scarcity of Western escort vessels and carriers for submarine-hunting helicopters, the technical progress achieved in ASW against conventionally powered submarines might not be fully felt. Although the number of submarines available for raider warfare is less impressive than the total size of the Soviet submarine fleet may lead one to believe (see our calculations above), the West would still have to resign itself to a considerable loss of tonnage. On the other hand, there are good prospects for a gradual lessening of the submarine threat. Given the size and technical complexity of a modern submarine, replacement of losses by new construction is definitely more time-consuming than it was in the Second World War.

The foregoing statements relate to the present period. To measure the future, a different yardstick is needed. The time when one had to reckon predominantly with conventional submarines is drawing to a close. As soon as the Soviets have refashioned their submarine fleet—retaining the quantity but shifting almost exclusively to nuclear propulsion—the threat of raider warfare is going to become very serious. Given the West's extreme dependence on shipping, the possibility of the U.S.S.R. achieving a decisive turn of the war by raider warfare alone cannot be ruled out. If the ASW technology of the time does not provide a more effective defense against nuclear submarines, the West will be tempted to have recourse to atomic depth charges. In taking such action, it would accept that the Soviets respond by using tactical atomic weapons themselves. This would raise the specter of a mortal threat against Western aircraft carriers, since submarine torpedoes and antiship missiles from aircraft and submarines, all equipped with nuclear warheads, would be likely to be directed towards them.

The Soviets are still far away from this stage of development. With their present nuclear-powered attack submarines they have reached only an intermediate phase. But the threat of raider warfare grows rapidly. We will return to these prospects in the chapter on Soviet naval forces in the future.

5

the role of soviet naval forces in peacetime

Maritime strategy and the atomic balance

In this era of atomic balance, new forms have evolved for applying military force below the threshold of open war. There are numerous variants: war by substitute; dispatch of advisors, "volunteers," or even regular troops to support allies; kindling of national "liberation" wars; and armed subversion. However, all these schemes lend themselves to application only on land. There are no analogous or truly comparable developments at sea. One would hardly have a chance to practice such distortions of international law on the high seas and remain inconspicuous. Surface ships cannot disguise themselves while engaged in combat. In almost all cases one can recognize the nationality of a surface ship from its flag and type or from the location and circumstances of combat. In part, this is true even of submarines, especially of conventional ones that can be forced to surface after a certain period of pursuit. Application of force at sea in peacetime—be it an action against civilian shipping, or some other military action—will be instantly known the world over, and will entail political consequences. *A fortiori*, political consequences will be even more serious if force is directed by one warship against another. It may be possible for second- or third-rate countries to commit, in isolated instances, acts of force against one another (or, at the behest of and for one world power, even against another world power, as, for example, in the *Pueblo* incident) without endangering world peace. But neither of the two superpowers can afford to have recourse to arms at sea in time of peace, in order to impose its will upon the other. Under the umbrella of the atomic balance, such an act of force by one warship against another could well set in motion the spiral in which the threshold of war would be attained.

We will, therefore, work on the assumption that the two superpowers will do anything to avoid the use of force by their warships against warships of the other side. It is *on the basis of this premise* that we will examine the role of Soviet naval forces in time of peace. For the moment, we will not take into account the important psychological effect of that premise or the political effect resulting therefrom. We will first examine the *effective military acts* that the navies of the two superpowers could afford to undertake in peacetime under the constraints of the atomic balance.

In times of peace, fighting ships are free to cruise in international waters as they see fit. They may stay there as long as they please and conduct whatever maneuvers they please. Nobody prevents them from getting into the vicinity of fighting ships of the other superpower with the intention of disturbing and molesting them, even though they be in violation of international usage.

But that exhausts the possibilities of military action on the high seas in peacetime, if international law is to be respected. Naval forces have no other legitimate means at their disposal, particularly for carrying out their inherent task of "controlling" the shipping lanes.

In spite of these tenets, there have been instances in the postwar period where naval forces—in breach of the law of the seas, to be sure—were employed against civilian shipping in peacetime. The most striking example is the Cuban blockade.

What about such use of the naval instrument? What are the particular conditions that make it possible? In order to acquire some concepts and principles for judgment, it appears useful to include here some considerations of a general nature.

Stopping and searching merchant ships and, if deemed necessary, seizing or sinking them, are acts of military force and are defined by the law of the seas as grave violations of law under peacetime conditions. If an *unarmed* merchant ship is thus "seized," there is no danger of physical counteraction. Escalation in the use of arms will not ensue. If seizure becomes a continuous practice, a blockade exists. If a blockade is announced beforehand and is supported by any military means to speak of, it is very likely to be effective in peacetime. Merchant ships will turn away or avoid the blockaded area altogether.

The situation is different when the merchant ship is escorted—even in peacetime—by a fighting ship. The merchant vessel may then disregard the threat of force and continue its voyage. The blockading vessel, if it insists on stopping the merchant ship, must fire the first shot, which the escort vessel will forthwith return. Naval combat has started. Accordingly, seizure of escorted civilian ships implies armed action of fighting ships against one another, the very situation both superpowers must avoid. We may conclude that in the era of the atomic balance seizure of the adversary's escorted shipping is precluded. Yet, the escort system works only if escort vessels are available in time. In sea areas situated at a considerable distance from the home base, it can function only if fighting ships of one's own fleet are present to the same extent as are the naval forces of the other side.

The conclusion is obvious: seizure is feasible only if the blockading side enjoys "lone presence." Simultaneous presence of the adversary—"counterpresence"—excludes seizure. Counterpresence neutralizes lone presence. In contrast with a wartime situation, the forces need not be balanced in all particulars. There is no intention to engage in battle. Presence and counterpresence are effective as soon as there are in the area enough vessels that are capable of firing the first shot or of returning it effectively.

From the viewpoint of military and political effect, presence is particularly useful when it is permanent. The concept of presence therefore implies duration. Permanent presence in waters remote from home bases make it desirable, or indeed—depending on the distance from the home base—necessary that a base be created nearby. The deployment period of modern fighting ships is dictated by technical factors. Some systems, especially propulsion systems, cannot be subjected to uninterrupted service at sea. Long periods in a particular sea area hence require provision for port time, during which all systems can be switched off. The better a port is technically equipped—berths with electrical outlets and water supply, repair shops, dockyards—the higher its value for peacetime presence. Availability of fresh water and fresh food, as well as relaxation for the crew, are equally desirable. Such harbor bases do not have to satisfy the requirements of a naval strategic position in wartime. It suffices that regular opportunities for entry and berth time are provided within the area of presence. We may refer to such bases as "maritime positions." Just as we defined sea power in war as the product of "fleet" times "naval strategic position," we take the product of "forces present" times "maritime position" as the yardstick of "maritime" power in peacetime.[20] The better the position, the longer forces present may be stationed. If the number of available ships is constant, a favorable position will also raise the density of presence. "Naval strategy" oriented towards war finds its equivalent in "maritime strategy" in peacetime.[21]

One should stress that seizure of seagoing traffic of the other side will be considered only as an expedient for the superpowers in rare situations of crisis. A breach of international law would in any case involve a serious loss of face before the worldwide audience and would entail, if not a setting in motion of the arms spiral, the dangers of political escalation. At the same time, it could initiate a spiral of reprisals. Seizure in an area of the world where one of the superpowers enjoyed lone presence could easily

[20] The definition of "maritime power" as the product of "forces present" times "maritime position" cannot claim the same universal validity as does our former definition of sea power (the product of "fleet" times "naval strategic position"), after which it is modeled. The reason is that a missing maritime position could, at great expense and at the price of various constraints, be replaced by seaborne supply. Even though the forces present without any land base may not represent full-fledged maritime power, one must acknowledge that they nevertheless exercise a certain degree of power. In other words, even if the factor value of "maritime position" goes down to "zero," the product may yet be greater than "zero."

[21] To employ the adjective *maritime* as a conceptual term for peacetime conditions is not quite in keeping with general usage. The author suggested this terminology in his article on "Theory of Naval Strategy in the Nuclear Age" (*Naval Review*, 1972). Since then, it seems to have found a certain acceptance as a useful tool for differentiating between "naval strategic" matters that relate to war and matters that relate to conditions of peace. Other authors have joined in using "maritime strategy" as a concept opposed to "naval strategy" (*see*, for instance, "Current Soviet Maritime Strategy and NATO," by M. Edmonds and J. Skitt in *International Affairs*, Vol. 45, No. 1). However, an overlap with a different usage of the word may be observed in British terminology. The Royal Navy applies "maritime power" to what we would refer to as "naval power," including the land-based naval aviation forces of the Coastal Command. This usage, which seems to flow from the special situation prevailing there, should not impede the terminology here suggested. Obviously one may continue to use the word *maritime* in its original larger sense as well.

lead to seizure in an area where the adversary had the monopoly of presence. Lone presence and taking advantage of it for the purpose of seizure could, in specific circumstances, have a determinant impact on world politics, as the Cuban blockade proved.[22] Whether Soviet ambitions to gain maritime presence are primarily and deliberately motivated by the corresponding opportunities for seizure—or prevention of seizure—is, however, questionable. Cases where seizure might become a significant option are too rare, after all. Yet, the concepts derived from a discussion of the seizure situation are quite useful. They make the situation at sea prevailing in time of peace particularly obvious.

However, if the Soviets do not aim at opportunities for seizure, one must seek further for the motive behind their huge effort to establish a maritime presence overseas and their policies in obtaining maritime bases everywhere. Quite obviously their objectives are of a political nature. The political effects that result from maritime power reside only partly in the inherent possibilities for actual military use of naval forces in peacetime. They are more clearly connected with the relationship between maritime power and sea power. Both these facets convey possibilities for propaganda and for the exercise of a psycho-strategic influence upon others. Let us first consider the relationship between maritime power and sea power proper.

Maritime power as a precursor of sea power

One of the prime prerequisites for a *naval strategic* position is a link with the sources of power and supply at home that would be safe in wartime: without such a lifeline, the position would necessarily dry up as the war went on. A *maritime* position can do without this feature: it is to be of service to the forces at sea in peacetime, while traffic, particularly seagoing traffic, flows unhindered. The feature that distinguishes a maritime position from a naval strategic position is, then, the lack of a safe wartime link with the power source at home.

[22] In the Cuban crisis, the extraordinary circumstances were as follows: an act of strategic-atomic significance had been committed in the immediate power area of the United States, where there was the strongest possible presence of the U.S. fleet and where the Soviets had no counterpresence whatever (i.e., no Soviet escorts for missile transports).

To convert a maritime position into a naval strategic position, the primary task is to establish a link that can be safeguarded. If this cannot be done with a land connection, one must gain control over the sea area between the position and the home country. In case of success, maritime power can be transformed into sea power, the extent depending on the strength of forces present, or forces then added, and their ability to form a factor "fleet." The transformation of maritime power into sea power could indeed be the real objective behind a strategy of gaining maritime bases and could possibly be the determinant motive for maintaining a peacetime presence of naval forces overseas.

Where the Soviets had no chance at all to convert positions in this way, or where conversion failed—in other words, where control over the route home would, in war, remain with the West—Soviet maritime positions in their resulting isolation from the Eastern Bloc would lose all their relevance for naval warfare. As of now, the host country of such base, in war economically dependent on the United States by virtue of its undisputed mastery of the sea, would have to bar its ports to Soviet naval forces. If it failed to do so because of faulty judgment or because Soviet occupation forces within the country exerted pressure, it would become practically a belligerent party. Failing political measures, the United States would soon enough apply force, be it to destroy Soviet naval forces then moored in the harbor, be it to force the host country to terminate such illegitimate support for the enemy's navy.

In sea areas where the geographical conditions for a conversion of positions exist, maritime power could be a precursor of sea power. Where such conditions are lacking, maritime power can have no relation to sea power and would be irrelevant in war. We must therefore distinguish between two kinds of maritime presence in peace. There is even a third one, namely the presence of naval forces in sea areas where the Soviets would never have so much as a chance to establish maritime position. Such physical presence of fighting ships does not qualify as a maritime presence under our definition. Again, this does not mean that warships dependent upon seaborne supply cannot travel to such areas for temporary stay. A presence of this kind, unless it were in sea areas near the home country, is not likely to be of any duration. One should bear in mind these different varieties of presence and their relative merits.

This section would be incomplete without a reminder of one grave weakness in Soviet maritime strategy. That strategy rests on positions in friendly countries, more or less dependent on the U.S.S.R. but with a sovereignty of their own. In case of a reorientation in such a country's internal or foreign policy, or if Soviet attitudes towards a given country, at first taken at face value as sheer altruism, should all of a sudden be recognized as thinly camouflaged expressions of imperialist expansionism, a rupture could occur. In fact, the host country could at any moment rid itself of the Soviets. Since the sea separates it from Soviet Bloc territory, it need not fear the vengeance of the Soviets or a Czechoslovakia-type of catastrophe. Such a government would have other options. It could orient itself towards the United States or lean towards the People's Republic of China. A good example for such reorientation is provided by Albania, which forced the Soviets to vacate their submarine base at Valona.

These facts indicate that a maritime position, once established, is always exposed to risk. Only an overseas base under one's own sovereignty is truly politically secure. However, the Soviets could ill afford acquisitions of this nature, lest they deprive their propaganda for anti-colonialism of credibility anywhere.

In spite of these limitations, the Soviets have been generally successful in their maritime strategy overseas. They have announced their claim to equality with the United States and their role at sea; the fact that, as a continental power, they were not represented on the oceans before, has rather augmented the effect of their maritime strategy. At this stage, prestige is at stake more than anything else. But the Soviets aim higher. Their final objective is expansion of power.

A worldwide change of climate

Before dealing with the possibilities for peacetime use of naval forces, we should point out that, at least for the major powers, the margin of maneuver for such use has become narrower than it used to be. In the age of colonialism, fighting ships had an array of tasks to deal with overseas, if necessary by force. A list would start with the foundation of colonies and would include armed intervention and blockade at sea and the realization and safeguarding of economic claims and privileges. The world at large would learn of such military actions only many months later, if at all.

Modern means of communication being what they are and the former colonies being now independent states with a strong sense of identity, bound in with regional and global international organizations, the change of situation is indeed fundamental. These organizations and their member states are highly sensitive towards anything that even faintly resembles neo-colonialism. This sensitivity is primarily geared towards Western countries but, in spite of the widespread socialist tendencies in the third world, the Soviet Union's margin of action is not much greater. It must take care—particularly with a view to the People's Republic of China—not to get involved in "imperialistic" acts in contradiction to its own anti-colonialist and anti-imperialist propaganda. Thus, to a considerable extent, the omnipresence of a global audience restrains activities of fighting ships in peacetime.

Furthermore, all events in the third world are today influenced by the bi-polar East-West structure of the world. Any major military action by one of the superpowers would immediately provoke reaction by the other, be it by political means, by economic or military assistance, or by direct military intervention. As regards actual combat in the framework of limited war, the constraint is clearly felt: both sides must strictly avoid, on land or at sea, a direct confrontation at arms with the other superpower, lest escalation be set in motion.

If one takes a good look at relevant third world countries from this angle, one sees clearly how narrow the margin for the military use of fighting ships in peacetime has become. China, for decades the favorite training ground for employing warships in times of peace, has now become for both East and West a place of *noli me tangere*.

Since the U.S. withdrawal from Vietnam, very much the same can be said of Southeast Asia. African, Arab, and South American countries, let alone countries bordering on the Indian Ocean, are protected from the use of force by superpower warships largely by virtue of their own armament, their regional organizations, the United Nations, and, last but not least, the effects of bi-polarism.

However, despite all these constraints, the mere presence of fighting ships denotes an inherent capability for the use of military force. In critical situations, the forces present could be concentrated for a show of power off a country's coast, and political pressure could thus be brought to bear. Its effect would depend on the expectations of the country concerned: would the power demonstrated off its coast be put to use or not? The country would also ask itself what the effective possibilities for the alien naval forces were, if they did indeed choose to intervene. To make an evaluation possible, we, too, should therefore ask ourselves where the possibilities would lie, taking into account the aforementioned constraints on their exercise.

Sea-based air power is the most effective instrument for the exercise of military might from the sea. Its effects go far beyond the coastal zone, covering the entire hinterland. Their present lack of aircraft carriers would thus prove a disadvantage to the Soviets with respect to the peacetime use of their naval forces. The argument that this fact contributed to the Soviet decision to build carriers, has some force, but it was surely not the primary motive.

The impact of sea-based artillery is limited to a fairly narrow coastal zone. The Soviets have no ships with heavy-caliber artillery. Modern Soviet missile cruisers and destroyers do not possess even medium-caliber gunnery. Intervening with ship-to-ship missiles armed with conventional warheads would make little sense; there is no precise targeting when one shells a coast.[23] The landing of troops would constitute a different kind of application of force. However, even in underdeveloped countries, such military intervention would nowadays require relatively large and well-equipped units. A landing force hastily constituted of sailors from fighting ships, as was frequently used even at the beginning of the century, would not accomplish anything anywhere because it would be insufficiently equipped and trained.

Bringing in troops ad hoc from the home country of the

[23] This does not exclude the firing of a missile at random and corresponding damage in densely populated residential areas or crowded harbors, because of the size of the explosive charge.

aggressor has nothing to do with "presence." Maritime presence could only be used in this sense if the forces present included amphibious forces with troops permanently embarked. There are definite limits for such long-term embarkation. The Soviet squadron in the Mediterranean has only a few amphibious vessels regularly assigned, and they have troops aboard only occasionally. Nor does the contingent of Marines permanently assigned to the U.S. Sixth Fleet exceed wartime battalion strength. The Soviets are not likely to have substantially higher numbers of troops permanently stationed in any particular sea area. One should add another aggravating factor: their amphibious ships are not designed for service in remote sea areas, in view of their limited operational range. They do have one large-size model, but only a few specimens of it are in existence.

Besides, one must assume that the Soviets are loath to dispatch the majority of their amphibious craft into remote sea areas on a long-term basis; in case of a large-scale war, they could hardly expect to get them back in time, or perhaps not at all. For strategic reasons, they would prefer to have these forces available in their own naval districts, since they play a decisive role in their offensive concept in the peripheral seas. All this means that a major military action in peacetime—e.g., invasion of a country accessible only from the sea—would have to be initiated with Soviet territory as the starting point.

Our analysis, then, shows that Soviet naval forces are not very well suited for military use overseas—less so, at any rate, than U.S. forces with their aircraft carriers, artillery-equipped ships, and oceangoing amphibious forces.

We have clearly seen that active application of these instruments against countries of the third world in violation of their sovereignty can, today, largely be excluded both for the Western industrialized countries and for the Soviet Union. Yet, there are cases where naval forces could be brought to bear in peacetime, the most likely being where a naval power is called in by a legal—or illegal—government, perhaps on the basis of an alliance treaty, to lend support against an interior political foe, against infiltration, or against subversion. Conceivably, that bid for assistance would only appear to stem from the local government, and would, in reality, stem from the intervenor country, by means of pressure or intrigue. The true purpose of the intervention could then be to keep a government in place, in keeping with the wishes of the intervenor, but contrary to those of the majority in the country concerned. If one thinks of such examples, it could well be that the Soviets could use an expansion of their maritime presence in an attempt to broaden the Brezhnev doctrine into a global concept. The possibility that the Soviet Union will use the instruments of maritime power to consolidate or reinstate a Moscow-leaning regime in a socialist country overseas should not by any means be ruled out.[24]

Limited war overseas

Active intervention on the basis of an appeal for support may lead to an involvement in combat on land, and even to participation in a limited war. There is no need to draw a picture of limited war: the Korean and Vietnam wars are examples of one type, and the Israeli-Arab wars are examples of another.

What is the role of maritime power in wars of this scope? Direct participants may fight not only on land, but also at sea. Although their status under international law and under the law of the sea may not be fully defined, their behavior will be similar to that usually practiced in an openly declared war. Between the superpowers, peace continues to reign, at least formally—a state of non-war. They are not directly involved in action against one another.

A superpower that had lone maritime presence in the area of the war theater could cut off essential supplies brought in by sea for the other side. If the other superpower appeared with counterpresence, the blockade at sea would come to an immediate end. Seizure would provoke instant counterseizure and the introduction of escorts.[25] That would, however, be the limit of what counterpresence could achieve. For if seizure and blockade at sea presupposes lone presence, participation in a limited war does not. If naval forces of the superpower that

[24] For example, one could have imagined Soviet intervention at sea in favor of Chile's late president, Allende, either in the form of a show of power or of active participation in the conflict. Apart from the presence of a task force, this would have presupposed advance preparations for the transport of troops and seaborne supply in the Southeast Pacific.

[25] Under favorable geographic conditions, a mine blockade would also be possible.

supported the "other side" made an appearance, the only thing that would have to be borne in mind would be the overriding premise that the superpowers must avoid a direct clash.

Each superpower could support its faction on land by shelling the coast, by use of carrier aircraft, or by amphibious landings—quite undisturbed by the other. The other superpower could quietly observe these military doings, if it so wished, or else do similar favors to the belligerent faction that it supported. But even though it were present with superior forces, it could not prevent by force what its superpower competitor was doing. Counterpresence and the capability of the other superpower to engage in similar activities might have only the indirect effect of discouraging somewhat the activities of the former.

In any case, support of land war from the sea can have considerable impact. Sea-based air power and amphibious operations on the flank of and behind the adversary's front could be decisive for the outcome. In view of this significant contribution which peacetime presence can make to limited wars overseas, some naval experts insist that this role provides the real justification of maritime presence and indeed the principal task of naval forces in the nuclear age. The present author, while fully aware of the significance of this kind of participation, is unable to share that view. A good deal of the political effect of peacetime presence arises from its interrelationship with sea power in a large-scale war. Justification for the fleets of the superpowers resides in the possibility of a large-scale war. All other uses of naval forces are of secondary importance. Besides, nobody can safely predict whether limited wars of the scope and character of the Korean and Vietnam wars will ever recur.

In conclusion, it is only fair to state that, so far, the Soviet Union has not used its maritime power actively in a military context overseas, either for seizure or to create a naval blockade, to intervene in breach of alien sovereignty, or to participate in a limited war.

The political effects of maritime presence

Accordingly, one may assume that, in practicing their maritime strategy, the Soviets aim less at the direct military effect than at the political effects that attach to maritime power. What exactly are these effects?

That political effects emanate from *sea power* even in peace is evidenced by the fact that the governments of countries that depend on the sea are clearly aware of the consequences resulting from sea power in wartime in the sea of their interest. The political weight of sea power is, so to speak, the credit accorded to the latent existence of sea power in peacetime. For example, the maritime presence of the Soviets can command only as much political credit as corresponds to its prospects of conversion into sea power in case of war. Where chances of conversion are good, or it can be assumed that they will grow, political credit is justified. In other areas of the world, where conversion can be ruled out, i.e., where Soviet forces in presence would disappear at the very outbreak of war, it is definitely not justified.

Obviously, for many governments it is hard to evaluate where chances of "conversion" exist and where they do not. They stick to what they see. And what they see is simple: where formerly only the British and the Americans had presence, there are now Soviet fighting ships as well; even more important, they see that the Soviets, for instance in the Indian Ocean, have replaced British ships and are present all by themselves. There is no doubt that this makes a political impact. Peacetime presence is not entirely explained, as theoretically it should be, by naval strategic arguments; the world, after all, does not obey reason alone. Psychological factors, difficult to predict and to measure, enter together with more tangible factors.

This goes beyond the field of naval and maritime strategy, which has so far been the subject of this study. Psychological "warfare" on ideological motives, in the form of propaganda and intoxication of the mind, are an integral part of the Communist system. They pave the way for Soviet foreign policy. Under the auspices of nuclear stalemate, where foreign policy excludes the possibility of war, psychological strategies have all but become the number one weapon of Soviet foreign policy. In an era when politics are more than ever influenced by public opinion, and public opinion itself can be influenced from outside more easily than ever, this weapon is highly effective, as evidence from any number of countries can show.

Soviet psychological strategy includes all phases of life. It goes almost without saying that the military sphere is particularly exposed to their efforts. Here they aim at making the world believe that the U.S.S.R. has become the strongest power on earth and is truly insuperable. The rapid growth of their strategic atomic potential serves this psychological objective just as much as do the superior capacity of their army and air force and, last but not least, the spectacular armament of their Navy.

More even than the other armed services, which are fettered to continental Soviet territory, the Navy is able conspicuously to display Soviet military might in all parts of the world. In the process, Soviet naval forces are designed especially to spread the impression that the West is now challenged in its very own domain of excellence, the control of shipping lanes on the oceans, and that the U.S.S.R. has set out, here as elsewhere, to outdo the West. This psychological motive is particularly evident from their worldwide naval maneuvers. For propaganda purposes, it is irrelevant whether they are based on realistic assumptions in terms of naval strategy. While such maneuvers do, of course, achieve genuine training objectives, their overriding purpose is often to impress world opinion, on the assumption that the world at large cannot judge whether Soviet fleets are operating in sea areas where they can appear safely, or appear at all, under conditions of war.

From a psychological standpoint it is totally irrelevant which one of the several varieties of peacetime presence is being displayed. It is true that Soviet maritime strategy is to a great extent founded on naval strategic reasoning; we will return to this aspect. The emphasis is indeed placed upon sea areas where chances of "conversion" exist, but it is not limited to these areas. Wherever Soviet maritime presence manifests itself, it is always closely interwoven with psychological strategy, of which it forms an integral part.

In order to achieve the psychological goals, it is necessary that the individual vessels present satisfy the claim that the Soviets put forward with their presence. There is an interdependence: the Soviet fleet is not built for psychological warfare, but for real warfare. Naval strategy and effectiveness in war are the essential objectives. But the psychological effect of demonstration flows from presumed effectiveness. In other words, if there were not a truly modern huge fleet behind it, a demonstration of peacetime presence would not generate a strong political effect.

This is one of the reasons why the Soviets do not construct their ships especially for peacetime demonstration uses, concentrating, as it were, on "impressive appearance." They design their forces in clear anticipation of future combat. Their ships do not in any way serve the purpose of Potemkin's sham villages.

For military purposes, the combat value of individual ships in demonstrating maritime presence in peacetime is not important. They are not there to engage in combat. For psychological effect, on the other hand, a modern missile destroyer with its mass of weapons and equipment—as enigmatic as it is imposing for the outsider—or an aircraft carrier with its enormous dimensions, is more impressive than, say, an oceanic research vessel. Yet, in its small way, even a research vessel fulfills a psychological mission, since it can be understood as part of the enormous Soviet fleet behind it.

Now, fighting ships cruising on the high seas are not visible to observers on land. Therefore, only when the forces in presence appear in ports and figure in reports by the mass media is the full psychological effect of maritime presence realized. Psychological strategy thus requires frequent calls in the ports of presence and prolonged stationing there. Again we note an interdependence: maritime positions are the prerequisite of maritime strategy; at the same time, they are important for psychological strategy. The better the psychological effect on an appearance in port, the better the political impact and, by the same token, the more firmly entrenched the position in the host country.

The psychological effects of Soviet peacetime presence are strongest where the Soviets are already hailed as keepers of the socialist faith and fellow fighters against colonialism and imperialism. The Americans cannot hope to match this. In a psychological climate deliberately created by the East, American peacetime presence in some countries of the third world may rather be counterproductive. Vilified from the outset as imperialists, racists, and world policemen, the United States has to display prudence in many countries, particularly in Africa and the Middle East. Americans must face up to the fact that their presence will not be acknowledged at its real value, which is to constitute a stabilizing counterpresence to the maritime presence of the Soviets.

A final remark in this connection may remind us that a mere "showing of the flag" may also contribute to the objectives of psychological strategy. Naval visits, as the Soviets practice them in large parts of the world, even where one cannot speak of maritime presence, work in this direction. For when a strong naval power shows its flag, an implicit show of power is involved. The entire weight of the sending state is put behind the flag, and commands respect. This effect is further amplified by the growing commercial fleet of the Soviets, their flotilla of fishing vessels, their oceanic research vessels, and their electronic intelligence ships. All of these show the Soviet flag and contribute to the representation of the U.S.S.R. as a seafaring nation of global importance.

Our general discussion on the concept of maritime presence may thus be concluded. With the definitions and points of reference obtained in the process, we may now turn to the role of Soviet naval forces in peacetime in various sea areas.

Soviet maritime presence in the Mediterranean

Moscow's peacetime offensive at sea—to the extent that it goes beyond the sea areas immediately adjacent to the Soviet coast—is most conspicuous in the Mediterranean. This sea lends itself extremely well to a maritime offensive. It is situated close to the center of Soviet power. Passage through the Dardanelles in peacetime by surface ships is practically free, even if the Treaty of Montreux is meticulously observed.

The Soviet maritime offensive in the Mediterranean started in the beginning of the sixties. From limited forces entirely based on seaborne supply, the Soviet Mediterranean squadron has steadily grown. In close parallel to their general increase of power in the Middle East, the Soviets established maritime positions in Syria and, above all, in Egypt. Even though Soviet "military advisors" have been expelled from Egypt, the Mediterranean squadron can rely on other Arab ports, especially in Syria. In the Mediterranean, the Soviets enjoy maritime power in the full sense of that term.

Earlier we considered what the naval strategic situation in the Mediterranean would be in time of war and concluded that the Soviets—if they broke open the Dardanelles and advanced their naval strategic position to the Balkan Peninsula—would stand a good chance of wresting sea power in the Mediterranean from the West. The Soviet squadron could thus play a precursor role for Soviet sea power in the area. This prospect, however it may be evaluated by individual Mediterranean countries, gives Soviet peacetime presence "credit" and conveys political weight. Soviet peacetime presence as such does not constitute a threat to the riparian countries or to the southern flank of NATO. The squadron ships have little possibility, in practice, of making

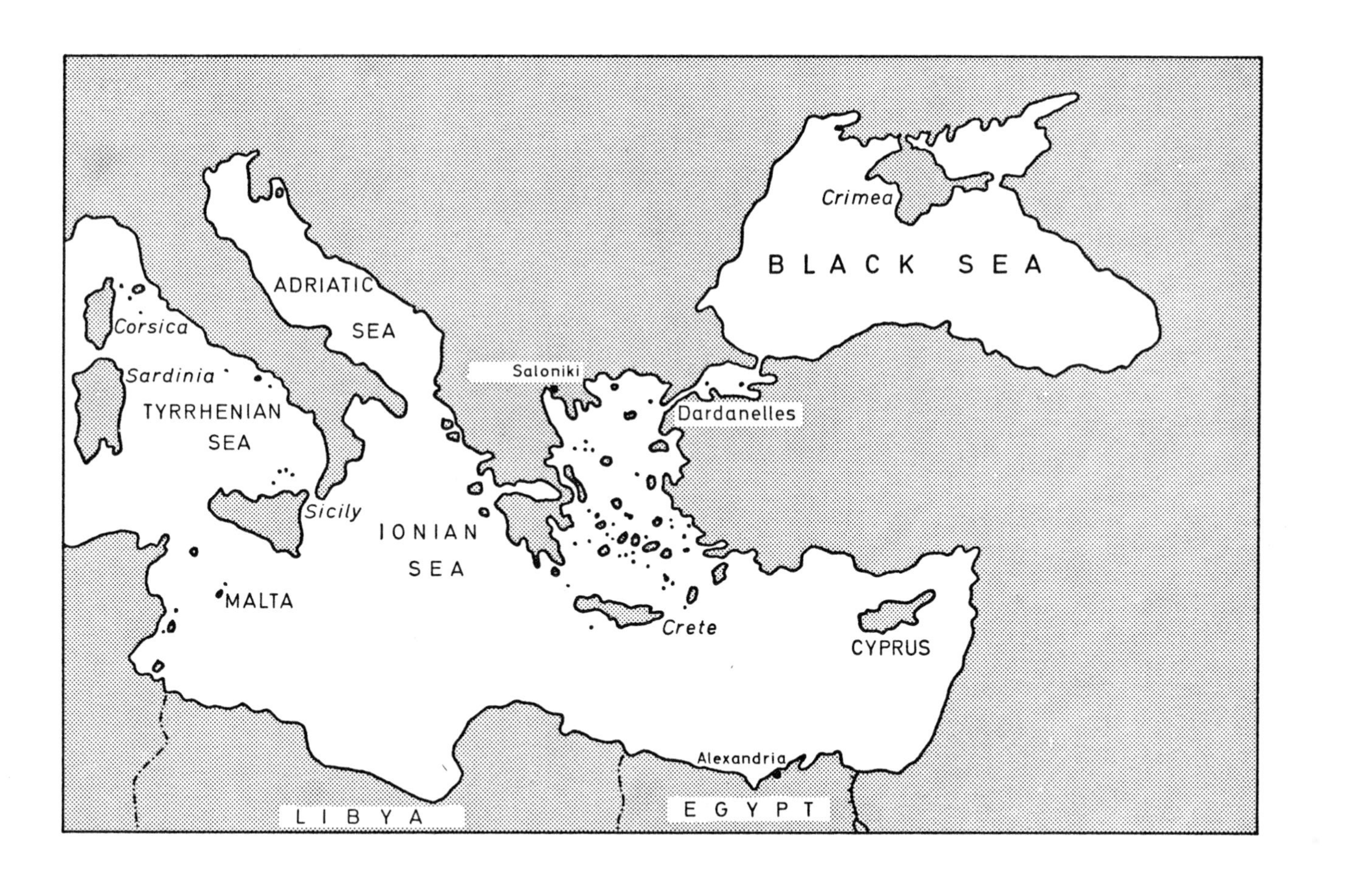
Crimea
BLACK SEA
ADRIATIC
SEA
Corsica
Sardinia
TYRRHENIAN
SEA
Saloniki
Dardanelles
Sicily
IONIAN
SEA
MALTA
Crete
CYPRUS
Alexandria
LIBYA
EGYPT

themselves felt militarily beyond the coastal strip of land. An amphibious action, conceivable as such, would not be a part of maritime presence proper, and would have to be carried on from the Black Sea area anyway.

Nevertheless, NATO's southern flank is threatened, but from the land side, not from the sea. This threat on land is not immediately visible, whereas the squadron is manifest to the eye. The threat is therefore primarily attributed to the squadron. In the short term, such attribution would not be justified, but in the long term it might be. Soviet peacetime presence, prefiguring Soviet sea power as it does, implies an obvious Soviet interest in the Balkan Peninsula as a potential naval strategic position. The Soviets may even now be casting covetous glances at it.

In the logic of naval strategy, then, seizure of the countries that form NATO's southern flank is a prerequisite of Soviet sea power rather than its objective. In reality, Soviet naval strategy aims at the Middle East and the Indian Ocean. In the Middle East, an area which it would be difficult for the Soviet army to reach under present circumstances, maritime presence in peacetime with its inherent chances of "conversion" properly carries a particular political weight. Its effect is accordingly stronger there than anywhere else.

Soviet peacetime presence in the Mediterranean has multiple political effects:

–It gives the Soviet Union the status of a Mediterranean power entitled to take part in the discussion of all Mediterranean issues;

–It neutralizes the U.S. Sixth Fleet as regards possibilities of "seizure";

–It demonstrates Soviet power to the Arab countries of the Mediterranean;

–It constitutes a counterweight to the U.S. Sixth Fleet in situations of crisis in the Mediterranean region, and may be used as an instrument of crisis management.

To explain the last-mentioned effect, a brief word on how maritime power could contribute to crisis management overseas is in order.

At sea, fighting ships might control a crisis by seizure; the Cuban crisis is a case in point. However, crises in which such solutions suggest themselves are rare. Crises on land are more frequent. Here one might bring one's influence to bear by dispatching a highly impressive task force of fighting ships into the crisis area, or by fortifying the forces already in presence. This might underline one's firm determination to protect one's interest. Behind the demonstration of these fighting ships, the entire power potential of a superpower would stand ready. Yet, the show of determination would be even more impressive if the task force were really capable of intervening rapidly and actively, if necessary. Conversely, the demonstration of resolve would be less credible or perhaps even irrelevant, if the task force, because of obvious political circumstances or because of its composition, was manifestly inappropriate for the occasion, and had no real ability to intervene.

In this sense, participation of aircraft carriers proves to be particularly persuasive. A similar effect would be created by fully manned amphibious units; these, however, as we have seen, the Soviets do not have present anywhere overseas in impressive numbers.

Given today's airlift capability, troops can be quickly brought in by air, provided that suitable airfields are available in the area of the faction to be supported. The airlifting of troops is, however, a more far-reaching step in crisis management than a demonstration at sea. The latter has the advantage that one may remain in international waters, even for an extended period of time, without being directly involved, while still creating a "menacing" effect.

From these considerations we may draw the following conclusions regarding the management of crises in the Mediterranean, especially in view of the Israeli-Arab conflict:

—The U.S. Sixth Fleet is better suited for a show of determination at sea than is the Soviet squadron. It possesses carrier-borne air power. Its ability to rush in sufficient numbers of troops is limited; they would have to be airlifted from elsewhere. An effect could, however, be made by the mere announcement that troops in the United States were being mobilized and shipped, in spite of the lapse of time between announcement and arrival.

—The Soviet squadron, on the other hand, is hardly in a position to intervene directly in events on land. A Soviet demonstration of power at sea could not therefore have an immediate effect. Yet, in the special circumstances that pertain in the Mediterranean, it could still constitute a signal of resolve. The home base is situated so close to the Mediterranean that troops and military equipment could quickly be brought in by sea or by air. A demonstration at sea would thus indicate the general determination of the Soviet Union to intervene. As soon as the airlifting of troops had started, such a demonstration would, of course, become superfluous.

In remote overseas areas, a Soviet show of power at sea would be unable to produce such indirect effects. Everything would depend on the capability of the forces in presence to intervene.

Soviet maritime presence in the Indian Ocean

The peacetime function of the Soviet squadron, and indirectly of the Black Sea Fleet, is not limited to the Mediterranean. To the extent that the Suez Canal is open for peacetime passage of fighting ships, Soviet presence in the Mediterranean becomes the permanent link with Soviet presence in the Indian Ocean. During the years when the Suez Canal was closed, the forces for Soviet maritime presence in the Indian Ocean were weak; most of them were provided by the Far Eastern Fleet. In the future, they will be largely increased from the Black Sea Fleet, certainly at the expense of the Mediterranean squadron. That need not diminish the political effect on the squadron. The forces present in the Indian Ocean and in the Mediterranean will form a whole, inasmuch as they have a direct connection, via the Red Sea and the Suez Canal; forces can at any time be moved along that inner line. Depending on situations and needs, they may show up in either the Indian Ocean or the Mediterranean. They have an impact in either sea, and thereby double their political effect.

Because of long-term preparation, the Soviet Union has a complete network of maritime positions in the northern part of the Indian Ocean, including its peripheral seas, the Red Sea and the Persian Gulf. By contrast, the West, formerly in possession of a series of bases all around the Indian Ocean, has lost all its maritime positions in the northern part.[26] Soviet presence can

[26] The U.S.S.R. has built harbors at Ras Banas on the Egyptian Red Sea coast, at Hodeida (Yemen), at Berbera (Somalia), at Umn Qasr (Iraq), and at Vishakhapatnam (east coast of India). Some of this construction started in the early sixties. This furnishes an indication of the long-term nature of Soviet maritime strategy in the Indian Ocean. Presently, Soviet forces in

therefore have an increased psychological and political effect, whereas the temporary presence of stronger U.S. task forces in the vast spaces of the northern Indian Ocean would go unnoticed, because they do not have maritime positions in the riparian states. The U.S. presence would have only minor effect.

The Indian Ocean provides a good example of the prerequisites for converting maritime positions into naval strategic positions, and maritime power into sea power. As long as the threefold barrier between the Eastern Bloc and the Indian Ocean (the Dardanelles, Western sea power in the eastern Mediterranean, and, as a consequence, Western control of the Suez Canal) is maintained, Soviet positions in the Indian Ocean will remain nothing more than maritime positions. Under those circumstances, Soviet naval forces that found themselves in the Indian Ocean at the outbreak of war would be doomed to "dry out." At most, they could hope to control a limited sea area around their positions; they would not be able to exercise mastery of the sea. If the war were to last for any considerable time, they would be in a hopeless situation, in spite of their numerous maritime positions. Cut off from the other Soviet naval districts by virtue of Western mastery of the sea in the Atlantic and the Pacific and with no Soviet commercial shipping in the area, Soviet forces present would have nothing to do but wait for a superior Western task force to do away with their surface units. In order to escape this unhappy fate, they would probably vacate the Indian Ocean before the way home was cut. After the West had thus established full control of the Indian Ocean, no riparian state would be able to escape the results of

presence call most often at Berbera and Umn Qasr. The port of Aden is also open to them. For many years, the Soviets have tried to obtain harbor rights in India and, in view of the closer ties with India that have recently developed, they may be successful some time in the future.

When harbor rights for the U.S. Navy in Bahrein run out, the only ports the West will have in the Indian Ocean will be in the southern part of it. The British island of Diego Garcia, strategically situated in the center of the Indian Ocean near the equator, is not a Western naval base—contrary to reports in the press—but merely a telecommunications and monitoring station operated jointly by the British and the Americans. There are plans to establish a naval base there. This could indeed remedy the present calamitous situation but, before it could be done, technical, climatic, financial, and, last but not least, political obstacles would have to be overcome, to say nothing of the manning problem. Perth and Fremantle, on the southwest coast of Australia, are too far away from the northern part of the Indian Ocean—even farther than Subic Bay, the U.S. naval base in the Philippines—to serve as remedies.

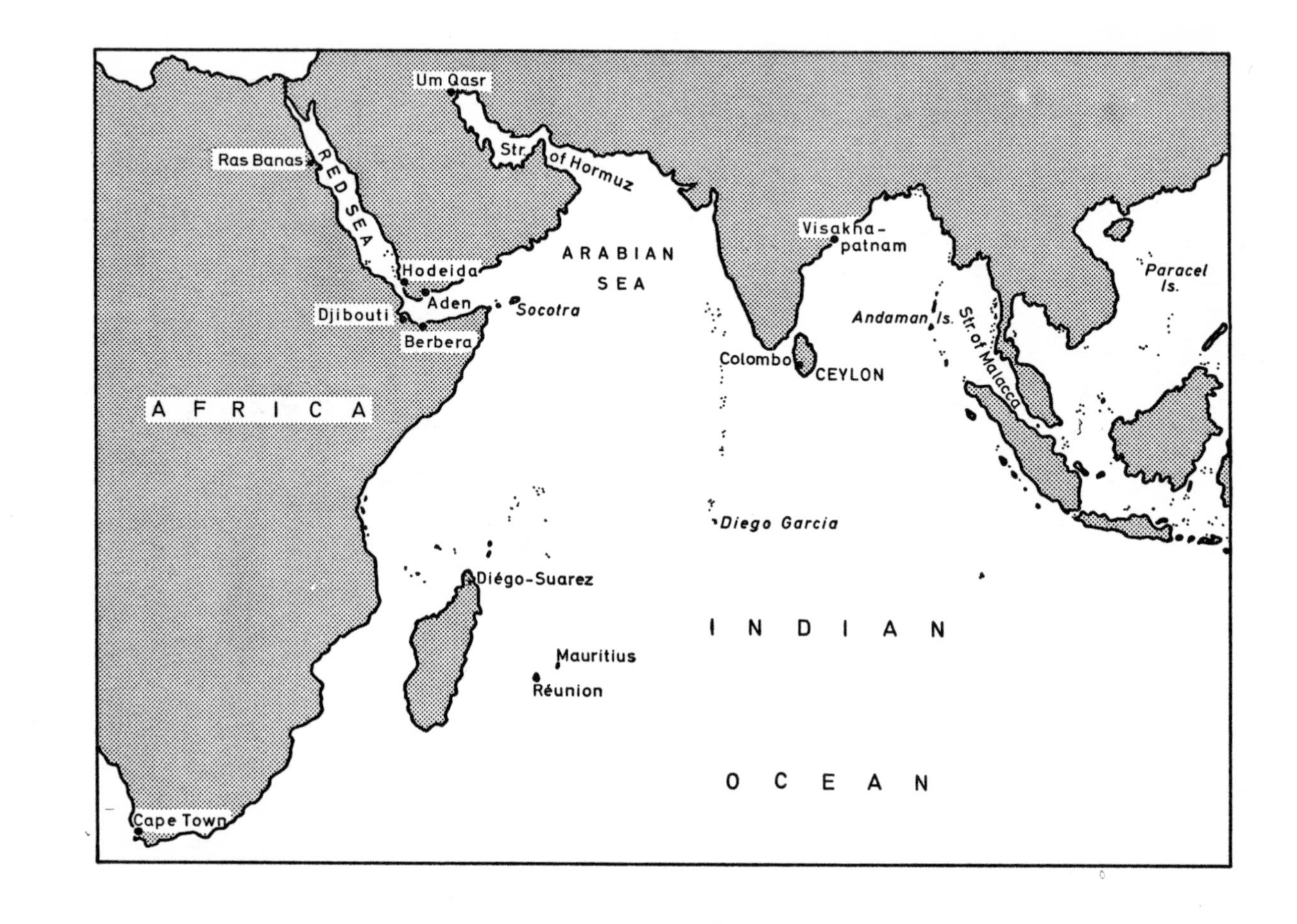
Um Qasr
Ras Banas
RED SEA
Str. of Hormuz
Hodeida
Aden
Djibouti
Berbera
Socotra
ARABIAN SEA
Visakha-
patnam
Paracel Is.
Andaman Is.
Str. of Malacca
Colombo
CEYLON
AFRICA
Diego Garcia
Diégo-Suarez
INDIAN
Mauritius
Réunion
OCEAN
Cape Town

Western mastery of the sea, no matter what its previous political orientations had been.

Conversely, if the Soviets should succeed in eliminating the threefold barrier, the Indian Ocean and the Eastern Bloc would be connected and Soviet maritime positions would be transformed into naval strategic positions. The Soviet positions in the Mediterranean and in the northern part of the Indian Ocean would become one huge overall position that would embrace the Arabian Peninsula and could, if maritime expansion continued, later include the positions on the west and east coasts of India. On this immensely broad maritime position sea power could be developed, depending on the available forces at sea, underwater and in the air space above the sea. That would allow the maritime presence in the northern Indian Ocean to be transformed, under the circumstances of war, into limited mastery of the sea. Thus, Soviet mastery of the sea in the eastern Mediterranean signifies much more than a mere threat to the southern flank of Europe and to the Arab countries.

In reality, the eastern Mediterranean is a sea area of decisive importance in the East-West confrontation. Naval strategic developments in the Indian Ocean and, as a consequence, political events in East Africa and in the Middle East, with its oil and population resources, hinge upon the future of this sea area.

Soviet maritime presence in other ocean areas

As we have seen, the chances for converting maritime power into sea power proper are particularly favorable in the Mediterranean and the northern part of the Indian Ocean. As long as present power conditions in terms of naval strategy prevail, the prerequisites for such conversion do not exist in other sea areas. This is notably true of the northern Atlantic. In this sea area, entirely circled as it is by NATO countries, the U.S.S.R. cannot find a hold for establishing maritime positions. When Soviet fighting ships sojourn in the northern Atlantic, they do not constitute "maritime presence," because the element of duration is lacking. No matter how much Soviet naval maneuvers in the Atlantic are expanded in space and time, when they are over the ships steam home and leave the northern Atlantic as it was before. It is a different thing altogether that the Soviets make good use of these maneuvers in their propaganda and that psychological effects emanate from this propaganda, even in the West. As long as U.S. aircraft carriers are ready for action and guarantee mastery of the sea in the northern Atlantic in case of armed conflict, the appearance of Soviet naval forces in that area in peacetime has no relevance in terms of naval strategy.

The situation is quite similar in the central and southern Atlantic. Even though the Soviets have acquired, or will acquire, maritime positions in the area, peacetime presence would collapse in case of war. Under the pressure of Western mastery of the sea, positions would be taken back by the host countries. This is equally true of West African and Latin American countries. There would be no chance of "converting" such presence.

A potential Soviet maritime base in Cuba would be no exception. In case of conflict, a base just off the U.S. coast would prove totally useless; the forces of presence would be retracted long before hostilities even started. If a Soviet base in Cuba is being used for strategic atomic submarines, as the press has written, these submarines can indeed extend their peacetime sojourn near their assigned firing stations. On the other hand, the deployment from Cuba of strategic atomic submarines would furnish the most convenient opportunity for the United States to shadow them.

Things are equally unfavorable for the Soviets in the northern Pacific, where the coasts of all riparian countries (the United States, Canada, Japan, the People's Republic of China) except their own are closed to them. The situation in terms of maritime strategy is quite similar to that in the northern Atlantic. As regards the southern Pacific, one can never rule out the possibility that a Latin American country might consent to grant harbor privileges to Soviet naval forces. In view of the vast distances separating it from the U.S.S.R. and of American mastery of the Pacific, such a position would again be useless in terms of naval strategic significance.

In the waters of Southeast Asia, a prognosis is less certain. One may safely rule out a restitution of the Soviet position in Indonesia. However, with the Vietnam war ended, it is hard to predict developments on the Indochina Peninsula. The question whether the Soviets can find a useful starting point for maritime strategy in the area is just as difficult to answer as the question whether the United States will be in a position to benefit in the long run from its bases in the Philippines (Subic Bay) and in

Thailand (Sattahip). One thing appears certain: developments in the South China Sea will have an influence upon the maritime situation in the Indian Ocean. Whether the Malacca Straits will remain an open international thoroughfare for fighting ships in peacetime, contrary to the wishes of Indonesia and Singapore, will be an important issue for both superpowers.

These glimpses permit us to draw a somewhat nuanced picture of Soviet maritime presence overseas: *From the viewpoint of naval strategy, it carries weight only where it could lead to Soviet mastery of the sea in war. This is the case of the Mediterranean and the northern part of the Indian Ocean. In all other areas, the effect has a psychological rather than a naval strategic dimension: the Soviets demonstrate power which will vanish at the moment of truth. Yet, the political effects of such presence should not be underrated.*

6

soviet naval forces in the future

Limits of a prognosis

Considerations of future possibilities naturally contain a speculative element. They cannot be free from uncertainty, especially in a field of learning such as the one that forms the subject matter of this study. Naval operations, naval tactics, and, thus, naval strategy are directly dependent on technology. The technology of naval armament, especially as regards ships, aircraft, and weapons systems, is rapidly advancing. Note must be taken of constant changes. The uncertainty factor is all the bigger because many significant changes in the area of sensors, position-finding, electronic countermeasures, etc. are not visible from the outside. Military secrecy is enforced particularly on the Soviet side, but it is practiced in many technical areas within NATO, too. As generous as NATO countries, especially the United States, have been in providing information on new weapons systems to the public, they must, for their own security, keep small the circle of parties informed on other important developments. Consequently, an outside observer is often poorly informed on details of technological developments even on the NATO side.

With this kind of information shortage, it is not easy to justify making a prognosis. Nevertheless, we will attempt—with great caution—to point out at least some aspects of the future that do hold some claim to probability because they lie within the general trend of development.[27]

[27] This section is based partly on Dr. H. Feigl, "Neue technische Entwicklungen für die Seekriegführung." (Ebenhausen, West Ge many, 1974. Stiftung Wissenschaft und Politik.)

Nuclear submarines

Throughout this investigation, references to the changes in naval warfare heralded by the nuclear-powered submarine have run like a red thread. In evaluating the present state of affairs, such terms as *for the time being, still*, and *so long as* have to be used again and again, indicating that further far-reaching changes are imminent.

These changes will take place (1) when the Soviets have a greater number of nuclear submarines in service than they have today; (2) when they have the ability to build nuclear submarines of substantially greater speed than those they have today; (3) when they can build submarines that are substantially quieter; and (4) when their sensoring devices reach a level of quality comparable to the development in the West.

Let us consider the quantitative aspect first. Working under the constraint to produce as quickly as possible a strategic atomic submarine fleet at least on a par with U.S. Polaris submarine forces, the Soviets have rapidly expanded their capacity for building nuclear submarines. That is also of benefit for the construction of attack submarines. The tempo of construction will be further stepped up as the priority building program for strategic atomic submarines gradually runs out. By the end of the 1970s, the share of nuclear-powered submarines could well have reached 50 percent of the total Soviet fleet of attack submarines. In the course of the 1980s, it might reach 100 percent.

The Americans are not likely to be able to match these growth rates. In the United States, rates of construction are not determined by reactor-building or dockyard capacity, but by the defense budget. Lately, never more than 5 to 7 nuclear submarines have been authorized per year. Although it is intended to step up these figures in the future, one may safely predict that the present equilibrium in the number of nuclear attack submarines will be transformed into a numerical superiority on the Soviet side. In the past, the differences between the strategic situations of the East and the West made for a difference in the numbers of submarines needed. The United States possessed mastery of the sea, while the Soviet Union had to have recourse to raider warfare. As the areas where the Soviet Union enjoys mastery of the sea expand, that situation is gradually changing. Today, the United States also must strive to have the largest possible submarine fleet, particularly in view of the important duties of the nuclear submarine as a hunter/killer submarine.

As regards quality, speed is essential. We have already discussed the importance of superior speed for attack and trailing operations. Superior speed becomes a question of survival when a submarine has to extract itself from the pursuit of a hunter/killer submarine. Physicists hold that maximum theoretical speed of an underwater vehicle (submarine and torpedo) lies around 50 knots. In the short or medium run, nuclear submarines will probably attain this top speed. They will then have reached an insuperable barrier. The Americans are ahead as regards speed. Submarines of the *Los Angeles* class are even faster than destroyers. Having got off to a late start, the Soviets are still behind in propulsion technology. Nobody knows exactly where the lag is or how long it will last. It is, however, safe to assume that they will gradually catch up with the United States.

Next to speed, the emphasis is on noise level. While the Americans have gone about as far as present technological development allows, the Soviets lag far behind. Obviously no propeller-driven vehicle can be absolutely quiet while traveling at high speed.[28] The noise of the hull itself is, therefore, particularly important at idling speed when the propeller noise is low or near zero. Idling occurs specifically while waiting in narrows for enemy submarines. In any event, the quieter submarine enjoys a decisive advantage in an engagement between two submarines.[29]

Acoustic devices must be able not only to detect noise from enemy ships over great distances, but to provide exact data on the bearing from which a noise comes. The change in bearing per

[28] Considerable progress has been achieved in minimizing propeller noises. The lowering of propeller noises not only increases a vessel's own safety: it also makes it easier for a traveling vessel to register noises from other sources. This is especially important for a destroyer. The lower its own propeller noise, even when it is traveling at high speeds, the greater the distance across which it can detect and localize a submarine, or at which, if it is traveling slowly, it can remain unnoticed by a submarine.

[29] In propulsion technology, the principle of thermic circulation offers a solution. With nuclear submarines of older types, circulation pumps, which have to be operated full blast even when the submarine is traveling slowly, constitute the principal source of noise. Thermic circulation makes these pumps superfluous. The "internal noise" is further decreased by the use of turbo-electric propulsion which obviates the need for noisy transmissions. Other sources of noise can, with care, also be eliminated, and the entire hull is then lined with anti-noise insulation material.

unit of time is one determinant for the firing of a torpedo or missile. Information on the distance of the target is also essential. The length of the hull is used as the basis for sonar measurement; by taking a sonar device in tow, the basis can be extended in the interest of greater precision of measurements. Real-time identification of noise information is equally important. This requires a computer in which comprehensive information on the signatures of vessels from either side is stored. All these data must be available in an integrated information system for easy real-time reference. As of now, the United States has a considerable lead over the Soviets in these areas.

The situation with respect to submarine weapons systems is different. Soviet submarines of the newest type have antiship missiles that are fired from a submerged position on the basis of acoustic position-finding alone. Since propeller noises travel over vast distances underwater, the firing range of these missiles goes far beyond that of a torpedo. The United States lags behind in this area, as it does in the field of antiship submarines missiles in general.[30]

Finally, submarine missiles capable of intercepting helicopters from a submerged position may soon be developed. Although its firing would require periscope observation and therefore would involve some degree of exposure of the submarine, this new weapon might constitute a setback for the most promising aspect of ASW, the noiseless detection of submarines by helicopters.

Very fast nuclear submarines

Given these new, high-performance features, the nuclear submarines of the future may well take over duties as underwater escorts, provided their margin of extra speed is satisfactory. They will be capable of detecting and fighting attacking enemy

[30] It is not yet certain whether antiship submarine missiles will be able fully to replace the torpedo. A missile hits a target above water, not below the waterline, as does a torpedo. This means that the torpedo's impact at target is considerably greater than that of a missile, unless the latter has a nuclear warhead. Besides, antiship torpedoes could also be improved as to range and speed, and could get higher target precision by means of wire guidance. Finally, the growing capability of surface ships' antimissile defense (point defense weapons) might give the torpedo an edge.

submarines earlier than can surface ASW, and might be able to intercept such submarines before the protected object is fired at. Submerged hunter/killer submarines could thus protect not only Polaris-type submarines, but also surface ships and task forces. Some fast nuclear submarines could be assigned to a carrier force in addition to the customary destroyers and helicopters.

On the other hand, the value of hunter/killer submarines in their escort function should not be overrated. The area to be covered around and ahead of a carrier force for the purpose of effective protection is large and likely to grow as the advanced submarine weapons systems referred to above are developed. The escort submarine, after localizing an enemy submarine, would be supposed to advance towards the firing position of the latter, normally at high speed. It would thus give away its own position. The enemy submarine would gain the advantage of quieter motion. The roles of hunter and victim might suddenly be reversed. This difficulty could be met only by putting up a very large screen and assigning considerable numbers of escort submarines.

Accordingly, the U.S. problem in deploying nuclear attack submarines for escort duties lies in the availability of a sufficient number of submarines. If one considers that, in wartime, carriers as well as Polaris submarines would need escort protection and that convoys of merchant ships would also require escorting, one can easily form an idea of the enormous number of submarines that would be engaged in escort duties alone. In addition, there would be the need for hunter/killer submarines to shadow Soviet strategic atomic submarines, to man waiting positions along such access routes of Soviet submarines as the Scotland-Iceland narrows and thoroughfares in the Far East. Finally, the West would also require nuclear attack submarines for offensive missions in the Mediterranean, in the Norwegian Sea, in the Indian Ocean, and, last but not least, in the Atlantic, in the event that surface ships showed up in these areas.

Compared to the dimensions of the threat and to the requirements, the U.S. building program for nuclear submarines in recent years has indeed been patently insufficient.

The conclusion of our investigation is that the nuclear attack submarine has a considerable margin of development left. Its attack capability will rise and its immunity from ASW will be improved. At least in the short run, there are no significant new trends in ASW. In spite of helicopters and hunter/killer submarines, and in spite of escort activities of submarines, relative chances of the attacker over the defender will continue to grow, and, accordingly, new possibilities for the nuclear submarine will open up. On the rapidly changing scene of naval warfare in the future, the nuclear-powered submarine will play an increasingly dominant role.

Reconnaissance

The Soviet submarine fleet's chances in a fight against aircraft carriers would be basically dependent on reconnaissance. An investigation of the future possibilities of the Soviet submarine fleet must, therefore, be preceded by an analysis of what the reconnaissance situation will be in the future.

We have stated that as of now, in case of emergency, the Soviets would not be able to provide oceanic naval reconnaissance from their unfavorable geographic position with the aircraft they have at their disposal. It is true that they possess bomber aircraft for strategic atomic duties with an intercontinental range and a reported speed of 3 mach. Should they build this aircraft in a reconnaissance version and assign it to naval warfare, their reconnaissance situation could indeed be decisively improved. The geographic handicap, especially in the Atlantic, would be serious for such aircraft, also. They could reach the ocean only after long flights over NATO territory or across the Iceland-Scotland gap. Supersonic aircraft are not protected against ground-air defense or fighters. The air-to-air missile system, F 14/Phoenix, is fully effective against supersonic aircraft. As long as the carriers are in existence and combat-ready, this same danger will exist for Soviet reconnaissance aircraft over the oceans as well. This fact would make it impossible for the aircraft to maintain contact with target vessels.

Air reconnaissance, if it is to provide the basis for a systematic war against aircraft carriers, must, however, be continuous. A carrier can alter her position considerably in a matter of a few hours. If continuous contact is not maintained, this loss must be offset by more frequent identification of the position of the carrier. Large numbers of long-range supersonic reconnaissance aircraft would be required for this purpose.

Whether the Soviets will consider it useful to equip themselves with a fleet of such extremely costly supersonic aircraft, large enough for this task, is open to question.

Reconnaissance by satellite must be evaluated differently.[31] Satellites orbiting around the earth provide photographs (or infrared pictures) of a situation very much limited in time. Reconnaissance results that are available only after recovery of the satellite are useless for operational purposes because of the quickly changing situation at sea. Geo-stationary satellites, which relay their findings to the ground by television, would be the best solution for the purpose of continuous naval reconnaissance. But geo-stationary satellites cannot be placed at altitudes low enough to register the details necessary for naval operations; nor would their television transmission have a resolving power that allowed the identification of ships. Finally, it is also open to question whether submerged submarines can receive such transmissions. Radar or infrared responses that are quite possible even at high altitudes are not as such necessarily good enough for identification. If geo-stationary satellites have to be ruled out, satellites with a circular orbit might be of value, if their findings could be relayed by television in real time. To be sure, the precise determination of position and course of a target in the open ocean on the basis of such data would not be easy.

In reality, as far as the outside observer knows, none of the essential questions has been solved. But, as soon as satellites can provide satisfactory data for continuous naval reconnaissance, the prerequisites for nuclear submarines to fight aircraft carriers will be at hand. The latter would then be exposed to an enormous threat.

It is not, however, possible to make a full assessment of what the situation would be, if that were the case, without knowing whether such satellites could be destroyed in an emergency and how long it would take to eliminate them after the outbreak of a conflict or after confirmation of a newly launched satellite. In other words, how long would the Soviets enjoy the use of a comprehensive continuous situation picture in carrying out a Phase I operation?

We know that the Soviets have experimented successfully

[31] In 1973, 75 Soviet satellites, 34 of which were photographic satellites, were registered, while the United States used a total of only 26 military satellites in the same year.

with satellites that are capable of destroying other satellites. We do not know about the Americans. We may assume that they are technologically capable of doing the same thing. The expenditure necessary is not known, nor is the quantity of anti-satellites the Americans might have in case of need. However, for the future, one ought to credit the United States with the ability to keep at least key zones, like the North Atlantic, free from Soviet reconnaissance satellites.

If this assumption is correct, then knowledge about the situation on the ocean will again depend on aircraft reconnaissance. In the Atlantic, geography favors the Americans. It permits them to survey this area continuously. The Soviets are—as they were before the satellite era—largely excluded from similar surveillance. This will bring them back into a situation of operational disadvantage as regards the fight of their submarines against the carriers.

Nuclear submarine versus aircraft carrier

With these preliminary considerations in mind, let us revert to Soviet prospects for eliminating American aircraft carriers by means of submarines.[32] Their prospects might improve if they had submarines with capabilities practically the same as, or even superior to, those of the U.S. *Los Angeles* class. Such submarines, having speeds that exceed those of carriers, could approach the latter as soon as reconnaissance indicated their position. If comprehensive reconnaissance were available, it would, in principle, be no problem to bring submarines close to reported carriers, even across oceanic distances.

Tactical chances would also improve. With superior speed the nuclear submarines could, even when approaching from astern, move into any desired attack position. Multiple repetition of an attack would be possible. If the submarines were faster than the

[32] It may be noted that land-based supersonic aircraft with extended range could also be used in the fight against American aircraft carriers. If the Soviets were to equip their strategic, variable-geometry aircraft (NATO code name, Backfire) for naval warfare, they could extend their "first wave" beyond the peripheral seas to at least limited parts of ocean areas. In spite of the various handicaps these aircraft have, they would then present an added threat for aircraft carriers on the oceans. It is an open question whether the Phoenix system and point-defense weapons would be sufficient to overcome it.

carriers, they could attach themselves not only to the enemy's submarines, but also to enemy carriers. Once a nuclear submarine had detected a carrier, it could constantly follow in its wake, at a distance determined by acoustic perception of the carrier's screw noise. However, one should not neglect to state that pursuit by acoustic guidance can encounter difficulties resulting from water turbulence or water stratification; it is quite possible for the submarine to lose contact.

In principle, Soviet nuclear submarines could attach themselves to American carriers in peacetime and tail them constantly, possibly with relief guard. Under peacetime conditions, destroyers and helicopters would be powerless against them, if international law were to be respected. Even though an American submarine escort might be close by, it could not prevent the submarine from firing the first shot. Since the Soviet submarine is bound to be the aggressor, the escorting submarine could intervene only after a Soviet act of aggression had taken place.

If trailing were to become the rule and every carrier at sea were followed by at least one Soviet submarine, then the U.S. carrier fleet would indeed be in the utmost danger. The Soviets could then fulfill their Phase I task (a possibility which we have discounted under present circumstances); that is to say, they would be able to attack most of the American carriers in a one-stroke operation at the very outbreak of war.

The appearance of such a mortal threat to American sea power would lay bare a weakness on the side of the West. That could motivate the Soviets conspicuously to carry out the trailing in peacetime and to publicize it in order to attain political effects to their liking. On the other hand, they might forego these effects of continual trailing and, for the sake of surprise, limit it to a period immediately preceding a real coup.

One might ask whether the Americans would be prepared to put up with such an audacious threat to their carriers in a period of peace. They could declare that they interpret the presence of unidentified submarines in the vicinity of their carriers as an aggressive act, against which they were compelled to take armed action. What the Soviet reaction to such an announcement would be, beyond protest and propaganda, cannot be predicted. An obvious move might be to instruct their submarines to surface and show the flag if arms were used. The Americans could not possibly proceed further against identified Soviet warships. They could not single out submarines and treat them differently from the way in which they treat other Soviet warships that regularly accompany American carriers in certain sea areas. If a submarine surfaced, it would lose contact with the carriers, since its superior speed can be attained only underwater. On the surface, it could not hope to keep track of the carriers.

If the carriers were to escape destruction, one way or the other, at the very outbreak of hostilities, then the chances of fast nuclear submarines would decrease substantially. Their success in detecting carriers would depend on whether they had enough continuous reconnaissance. If reconnaissance failed, the chances of even fast submarines would be reduced to fortuitous encounters. Given the vastness of the oceans, a quick, total elimination of the American carrier fleet could not be expected, even if the Soviets mustered a large submarine armada.

However, should the Soviets successfully pull off a surprise attack on a great number of carriers at the very opening of a war, not only would Western mastery of the sea be jeopardized, but the situation of submarine warfare would be greatly changed. It would be possible to release all submarines of the "second wave" from their defensive duties in the peripheral seas, because the destruction of the majority of the carriers would make those duties pointless. The submarines would be available for raider warfare on the oceans. Phase II could begin with a maximum number of submarines.

Tactical naval air superiority would also be eliminated by the destruction of the carriers. Soviet missile cruisers and missile destroyers could then appear on the oceans, primarily on the Atlantic. Their ship-to-ship missiles would have a chance of eliminating American cruisers and destroyers, if there were an encounter. Beyond the area covered by land-based NATO naval air power, there would be no reason for the Soviets to keep their missile-ship task force together. Spread out, the missile ships could help to make Western shipping impossible.

It is doubtful, though, whether using them for such purposes would be worthwhile, compared to employing submarines. Missile ships would be an attractive target for fast U.S. nuclear submarines. One should also not forget that fuel supply might be a difficult problem for the missile ships, even if the U.S. carriers had been eliminated. Tankers, spotted from the air, would be easy targets for American submarines. Even in the situation pictured here, Soviet surface ships would not have a naval strategic position.

The overall picture of future developments, as described above, gives one the impression that the nuclear submarine and, to a somewhat lesser extent, land-based, long-range aircraft will dominate the scene at sea. For the surface ship and especially the carrier, the bell seems to toll.

This conclusion is obviously incorrect. Facts that can be adduced from either superpower, the United States and the U.S.S.R., contradict it. The U.S. Navy is holding on to the carrier concept: a fourth nuclear-powered super carrier has been authorized. And at this very moment, when such ships appear to be particularly threatened, the U.S.S.R. is embarking on the construction of aircraft carriers, something it had strictly refused to do since the time of Stalin's death.

In the United States, there is a full awareness of the dangers that the very fast nuclear submarine presents for surface ships, and especially for aircraft carriers. No one knows better than the U.S. Navy the possibilities that this fighting instrument offers. It has had the opportunity to gain actual experience with fast, quiet, nuclear submarines, by testing them in practical maneuvers to see how they withstand modern ASW measures and what potential they have for attacking surface ships and submarines.

This experience has obviously led many American naval officers to conclusions similar to those we have drawn here. In any event, the former U.S. Chief of Naval Operations, Admiral Elmo R. Zumwalt, Jr., saw good reason to go on record against an overly pessimistic evaluation of the future of carriers. He pointed to the fact that, in the course of the Second World War, the U.S. Navy lost only four large attack carriers; even the kamikaze flyers were unable to shake for a single moment American tactical naval air superiority in the Pacific War. In his view, even the major accidents that have occurred in recent years had demonstrated the resistance of modern American carriers. In one case, a carrier remained fully combat ready despite the explosion of two 1,000-kg. bombs.

However, this statement of the Chief of Naval Operations made no reference to the new dangers that carriers face today: the ability of fast nuclear submarines to trail a carrier and to attack repeatedly; the fact that submarines are now armed with missiles; and the difficulty of staving off such submarines. Nevertheless, his reference to the resistance power of carriers is certainly still justified: their ability to stay afloat even if hit by large-caliber conventional weapons is quite considerable. There is no doubt that they can also survive torpedo hits. In almost any case, however, the carrier would then be forced to suspend its operations and undergo lengthy repairs. When this happened, the aggressor would have fulfilled his mission even though he had been unable to sink the carrier.

In giving his optimistic judgment, the admiral was perhaps thinking of certain technological developments that are presently underway. They may change the picture and again improve the chances for surface ships to survive attacks by nuclear submarines. In the following section we will glance at such potential developments, limiting ourselves to those that are directly or indirectly related to aircraft carriers.

The aircraft carrier of the future

In the light of their high degree of exposure, the weakness of the U.S. Navy is the small number of large aircraft carriers it possesses. At the end of the war in the Pacific, the American Navy had 129 carriers: ten years ago, it still had 24 carriers—15 attack carriers and 9 ASW carriers. As a consequence of the ever-increasing size and weight of ever-more-effective types of aircraft, of attempts to carry the largest possible number of them, and of the fact that modern aircraft require much longer runways, the size of the carriers has increased considerably. In the process, the combat potential of each carrier increased, but the number of them in service fell off. By the end of the 1970s, the fleet of American attack carriers will consist of 12 ships, four of them with nuclear propulsion. In view of possible carrier losses, there are unquestionably too many eggs in one basket today. That makes a Phase I operation very tempting for the Soviets: the elimination of only one carrier means the destruction of almost 10 percent of American carrier strength.

On the other hand, a strong tactical naval air capability on the high seas will continue to be indispensable for the maintenance of mastery of the sea in the face of Soviet ambitions. The importance of this weapon will grow rather than diminish.

This problem can be solved only by building smaller carriers of which one can afford to have a large number. But smaller carriers necessitate smaller aircraft. In both East and West it is common knowledge today that the problem has to be tackled from the aircraft side, and that the trend towards ever larger and heavier, costly, multi-purpose, high-performance aircraft must not be continued.

There are various ways to achieve this objective. The most radical one would be to switch over to aircraft for which the size of the carrier platform is irrelevant, that is to say, to aircraft that take off vertically, be they fixed-wing VTOL aircraft or helicopters. Compared to current high-performance aircraft, VTOL craft so far developed are slow and do not have sufficient operational radius or payload capacity. However, it is expected that they will finally attain supersonic speed. For the helicopter, too, an increase of speed up to 700 km an hour appears a realistic possibility. Yet, although helicopters, besides their ASW capability, lend themselves to an array of other duties (reconnaissance, electronic countermeasures, missile defense), they can never fully replace fixed-wing aircraft.

Another possibility would be the construction of much cheaper, lightweight, single-purpose aircraft that could be developed into short-takeoff and -landing craft by means of special takeoff aids, e.g., thrust-augmented wings (STOL). Such "compact" naval aircraft could take advantage of the development of very advanced structural materials of high tensile strength and light weight, as have been successfully tested for use in aircraft construction by the U.S. Air Force.

Whatever such new developments might bring, it will be some time before V/STOL craft can match the performance of present high-speed aircraft. It would be possible to settle for aircraft of a lower rate of performance for combat over the oceans if both sides renounced high-performance aircraft. In attacking ship targets, an aircraft using stand-off weapons can remain outside the range of surface-to-air missiles and aerial combat. Accordingly, it will be superior sensoring equipment, as well as the range and precision of air-to-air missiles, rather than the speed and handling of aircraft, that will be of the essence. Operational radius and a payload factor that allows for a satisfactory sensoring capability and reasonable armament will, however, be indispensable for new types of carrier-borne aircraft. It is still uncertain whether V/STOL will be able to qualify in this respect.

Even if these requirements were met, such new developments would not be entirely devoid of problems. If carrier-borne aircraft lagged behind land-based aircraft, then the threat, already considerable, to aircraft carriers within the range of enemy land-based naval aviation would increase. Since the overall strategic situation at sea would require such operations primarily for U.S. aircraft carriers, the scaling-down of sea-based aircraft would put the United States at a disadvantage. For operations in such areas, the United States would have to rely upon high-performance aircraft and, hence, upon its large aircraft carriers.

Although the trend towards new types of carrier-borne aircraft has barely become visible, and although the final outcome cannot be foreseen, both the Soviet Navy and the U.S. Navy have to some extent acted in anticipation of the future. The Soviets have built an aircraft carrier of 30,000-40,000 tons, the *Kiev*, which has no catapult or arresting gear and is obviously designed for V/STOL craft and antisubmarine helicopters. Since a second ship of the same type is under construction, it is assumed that the Soviets plan on a series. The tactical value of these ships will largely depend on the performance of their V/STOL aircraft. At present, this is not known. A surprise is not to be excluded, since the Soviets are credited with a lead in V/STOL technology.

The Americans have started building a series of small aircraft carriers. These 14,000-ton "sea control ships" will have 14 helicopters and 3 V/STOL aircraft. As they are only sparingly provided with sensors and weapons, they will probably not be able to operate, or to operate by themselves, in sea areas where the enemy might attack. The missions to be assigned to this type of ship are to serve merely as escort vessels for the protection of convoys, as their name indicates; participation in the defense of aircraft carriers would necessitate a high speed, which they lack. Sea control ships will, therefore, not be able to replace attack carriers. If the United States is considering building other new carriers, they will have to think in terms of a ship more or less equivalent to the *Kiev* in size.

Making smaller carriers would solve only some of the carrier problems. Inferiority in speed to the nuclear submarine would continue to be a handicap. That is also true of carrier surface escort ships. Given traditional hull configurations, a considerable increase in the speed of surface ships is out of the question. The limit that cannot be exceeded at reasonable expenditure is 35 knots. Neither gas turbines nor nuclear propulsion change this state of affairs.

In order to return to the surface ship its former superiority in speed over the submarine, substantially higher speeds would be necessary. Theoretically, craft that attain such speeds can be designed. Hydrofoils are a case in point. They can attain 80 knots. Considerable technological progress has been made in recent years in both East and West in assuring the maneuverability of hydrofoils in rough water. Unfortunately, the hydrofoil principle lends itself to the construction of smaller craft only, since for larger ships the hydrofoil itself would have to be increased out of proportion. Hydrofoil ships are, therefore, conceivable for coastal areas only as fast patrol boats armed with missiles and torpedoes, or as submarine chasers.

Surface-effects ships, whose hulls are lifted above the water surface by means of an air cushion, do not have these handicaps. They could attain speeds of up to 100 knots. Two rigid sidewalls and curtains fore and aft prevent the air cushion from escaping. Surface-effects ships are built on the same principles as aircraft, lack stability when turning and in rough waters, and need complicated electronic equipment for regulating a system of pumps. One must wait and see whether, with such gear, they display seagoing properties sufficient for use on the oceans. Other unsolved problems include fuel-carrying capacity, vibration, and noise. The U.S. Navy has two 100-ton experimental craft, and two 2,000-ton experimental models now in the design stage. Optimists expect that the surface-effects principle may be applied successfully to ships up to destroyer and aircraft carrier size. This would indeed be a revolution in naval architecture, since surface-effects ships could then restore to the surface ship superiority in speed over the submarine. A healthy skepticism seems, however, indicated while developments go on.

Protection of aircraft carriers

Since the future does not seem to have in store a major change in the relationship between the carrier and the submarine, one may well ask whether there are any prospects for better protection of the carrier.

No substantial change is to be expected as regards screening destroyers. New destroyer types, as the Americans are now building them, will be quieter than their predecessors and will be equipped with more sophisticated electronics, including automation and long-range sonar that will be less affected by the ship's own speed· They are, nevertheless, bound to lose their role as autonomous ASW systems whose principal instrument is sonar. Their future cooperative role in ASW will consist of carrying helicopters and providing long-range AS weapons to be fired at submarines detected and localized by helicopter.

Older destroyers, especially to the extent that they do not carry helicopters, will increasingly lose their ASW capability. That holds true for Britain's frigates, which form the major part of the Royal Navy, and *a fortiori* for Soviet missile destroyers which were designed as outsized submarine hunters as part of the Soviet anti-Polaris strategy. Even in the most recent class of Soviet destoyers one fails to discover any innovation in the sense of a stronger ASW capability.

Thus, defending against fast nuclear submarines is not a task that can be entrusted to destroyers, even modern ones. Interest, therefore, is increasingly directed towards interception of submarine missiles, which, of course, includes interception of antiship missiles fired by bomber aircraft or surface ships. There is a joint defensive effort by carriers, destroyers, helicopters specially assigned for the purpose, and such carrier-borne fighter planes as protect the task force. Interception weapons include such long-range, air-to-air missiles as, for instance, the Phoenix, and short-range missiles to be fired from ships and helicopters. Radar-guided gunnery, which specializes in throwing the heaviest possible load of metal at the incoming missile, is also very promising. An indication of the chances of success which the Soviets attribute to this kind of defense weapon may be gathered from the fact that the *Kiev* has no less than 28 guns of 57 mm. Electronic countermeasures are also applied but they are, of course, effective only the very short targeting phase of the missile, which does not exceed 20 to 30 seconds. Modern electronic countermeasures attempt to provide radar-infrared decoy targets, onto which the homing devices of flying-on missiles lock.

The effectiveness of any measure for intercepting missiles depends on timely detection of the missile. If possible, the firing itself must be detected. Very-low-flying missiles, so-called skimmers, stay below the scope of ship radar. For spotting skimmers, the airborne component of the defensive system is of particular importance. Special anti-skimmer radar is being developed.

This kind of joint effort can function only with automatic relay of data and computerized data-processing capable of providing the situation picture in real time, identifying the most dangerous missiles, setting guidance systems, and automatically releasing the shot and the various electronic countermeasures at the appropriate moment.

An integrated electronic system of this kind would also provide the basis for the use of laser beams in close-range interception of aircraft and in antimissile defense, supposing that such a beam could be made effective enough to be used as a weapon. Since it would be difficult to provide from aboard ship the precise continuous guidance required by a laser beam, a laser-equipped helicopter could probably do the job better. Laser guns might, as a development of the further future, be able to destroy missiles with a charge of very high energy. Should such weapons become available, the problem of missile interception would be taken care of once and for all. This would also mean the uprating of surface ships, since only surface ships could generate the enormous energy required for laser guns.

Any of these systems of missile interception would, if effective, deprive the nuclear submarine of its most powerful weapon. It would have to revert to the torpedo, a weapon that necessitates getting much closer to the target, and hence implies increased exposure.

To summarize, there is some hope that the task of protecting aircraft carriers will gradually be facilitated as a result of ongoing technological developments. Since the Soviets have now embarked on carrier construction, they will find themselves confronted by the very same tactical and technical problems as the Americans.

Soviet aircraft carriers and naval strategic concepts

This leads us to the concluding part of this chapter, namely the decision of the Soviets to build aircraft carriers. The general line of Soviet naval strategy has, in the past, been not to confront the West and its naval forces with means of the same order. Their concept of getting around Western sea power with quite different weapons, weapons that did not even exist at the time the carrier concept was developed, has proved successful in the peripheral sea areas. For decades, the Soviets have been forced to resort on the oceans to the weaker form of naval strategy, raider warfare;

now at last the possibility of overcoming this handicap with the help of the nuclear submarine has come in sight.

By shifting their emphasis to large surface ships,[33] the Soviets are embarking on a course that is not without problems. They may develop the same weak spot in which they would like to hit the Americans, and that in a situation in which the Americans enjoy a lead as regards the strong weapon against large surface ships, the fast nuclear submarine. Soviet aircraft carriers are certain to provide especially tempting targets for American fast nuclear submarines.

What, then, can have motivated the Soviets to change so incisively their previous naval strategic concept? One might be tempted to guess that they are aiming primarily at increasing the psychological effect of their maritime presence in peacetime with the aid of aircraft carriers. Such an effect is doubtless to be expected when Soviet carriers, ships of considerable tonnage, appear on distant seas and in overseas ports. Military possibilities for intervention in land warfare from the sea would also be increased. Yet, these kinds of goals, even though they may have had a secondary voice in Soviet planning, are not likely to be the chief motive. All previous Soviet fighting-ship designs have been aimed strictly at combat use. The psychological-political effect of peacetime presence does indeed rest directly upon how effective Soviet naval armament would be in case of conflict. As we have concluded before, Soviet ships bear no resemblance to Potemkin's villages.

No aircraft carriers are needed for Soviet warfare in the peripheral seas. In the Baltic, the Black Sea, and the Sea of Japan, they would be not only unnecessary but actually unusable. Should aircraft carriers be added to the Northern Fleet, it would not be for combat in the Norwegian Sea. There, the forces already present are sufficient for the "three waves," and land-based naval aviation makes better sense than carrier-based aviation. The Soviet decision to build aircraft carriers is more likely to stem from an oceanic goal.

[33] The tonnage of newly built Soviet cruisers continues to grow. The most recent type, the Kara class, displaces approximately 10,000 tons in contrast to its predecessors, the Kresta and Kresta II classes with 6,000 and 7,500 tons, respectively. One may also point to the two ASW helicopter carriers of the *Moskva* class, which are outsized for their mission.

From earlier investigation, we know that Soviet missile ships cannot sojourn for long periods in the Atlantic and Pacific. This is not only a result of Western mastery of the sea. Lack of seaborne supply in an area controlled by the other side, the resulting dependence on remote homeland bases, the danger involved in passing the narrows, the problem of damaged ships—all these things place Soviet surface ships in a precarious position on the oceans. Even if carriers were to join the Soviet missile ships, and if they were to form the nucleus of task forces on the ocean, that situation would not improve. Supposing for the moment that the carriers had nuclear propulsion and were thus freed from fuel replenishment, the task forces as a whole would still be under the same constraint. Their presence on the ocean would lack the element of duration. An operation would still be no more than a raid.

Let us attempt to measure this state of affairs against the concepts of naval strategy. With the construction of carriers, the Soviets would indeed provide themselves with a "fleet." What they would even then be lacking in the Atlantic and in the Pacific is the second factor of sea power, "naval strategic position." Without it, they could not hope to establish oceanic sea power, even though their carriers might be competitive. In order to have sea power on the Atlantic, the U.S.S.R. would have to push to the ocean's coasts in Western Europe and simultaneously in North Africa, an undertaking they would have to pay for with a third world war. In the Far East, a naval strategic position on the ocean is not conceivable, even supposing they could make geographic advances.

Accordingly, Soviet aircraft carriers will be able to contribute to the formation of oceanic sea power only where naval strategic positions on the ocean can be made available. Only the Indian Ocean would seem to offer such possibilities. There, maritime positions could be converted into naval strategic positions, provided the threefold barrier—the Dardanelles, Western mastery of the sea in the eastern Mediterranean, and the Suez Canal—could be cleared in time. Based on such positions, Soviet naval forces, with the aid of aircraft carriers, could turn into oceanic sea power. In wartime, this could lead to Soviet mastery of the sea in the northern part of the Indian Ocean. Western shipping would cease, and Soviet shipping would flow from there to the Eastern bloc, via the Suez Canal and the eastern Mediterranean. This sea link would also allow for forces to be moved along the inward line in response to the situation at hand. A Suez Canal open to Soviet naval forces would contribute to the psychological-political effect of Soviet peacetime presence in the Indian Ocean. It thus appears that Soviet carrier construction is aimed primarily at the Indian Ocean. In this area, the deployment of aircraft carriers is an obvious and worthwhile step.

Soviet mastery of the sea in the northern part of the Indian Ocean would be a challenge for the West, in view of the enormous stakes involved. In order to contest it, the West would have to send superior carrier forces into the Indian Ocean—we have said this before—and overpower the Soviet carriers. The Americans would have to do this under the handicap of an unfavorable position, while the Soviets would be able to join the battle from a broadly spread-out favorable position. In this context it becomes especially evident what the destruction of American carriers in a Phase I operation would mean: Soviet mastery of the sea in the Indian Ocean would go entirely unchallenged.

Aircraft carriers could thus bring about a situation in which Soviet mastery of the sea could become a reality in at least one of the three great oceans. The eastern Mediterranean remains the key zone on which Soviet mastery in the Indian Ocean hinges. Whether positions in the Indian Ocean remain maritime or become naval strategic depends on this area.

Prospects are not rosy for the West. But, let us remember, the picture we have painted is partly hypothetical. American aircraft carriers are still in existence, American mastery of the sea on the oceans is still a fact, Soviet aircraft carriers are still not competitive, the Soviet submarine fleet is still without that preponderance of nuclear submarines, the Americans are still alone in having very fast nuclear submarines. But the fact that future developments such as those described here lie within the realm of possibility demonstrates what opportunities the East has and what dangers threaten the West.

7

final balance

World revolution and the Soviet quest for sea power

By their very nature, the different conditioning factors in the peripheral seas and on the oceans, in war and in peace, now and in the future, have made it necessary to present many particular sets of circumstances. In conclusion, we must attempt to put these pieces together in a comprehensive picture and arrange them in a larger context.

The ultimate goal of all Soviet politics and strategy was and is, unaltered and undisguised, Communist world revolution. From the beginning, this goal was not intended to be merely an ideological one. Lenin and others have openly declared that it can and should be reached only through Soviet Russian hegemony. World revolution is, then, identical with Soviet imperialism! A temporary setting aside of this goal, whether because of Soviet weakness or Western firmness, has always proved to be only a tactical maneuver. Beyond all shifts in Soviet politics and all changes in the world situation, the long-term goal remains fixedly Soviet hegemony over the world.

The route, the tempo, and the priorities may change at any given stage. Although, true to the continental tradition of Russia, the Soviet quest for hegemony focused at first on the European continent, worldwide ideological activity continued undeterred. Lenin, and after him Stalin, saw hegemony over Central Europe as the first and decisive step toward world revolution. Only with the political decline of Europe after the Second World War did the United States appear as the real opposite pole to Soviet imperialism. Then the idea grew among the Soviets that the path to world hegemony did not necessarily have to lead via Central Europe. The founding of NATO, providing a stop sign in Europe, pointed in the same direction.

Thus there came to the fore an element which, not being in keeping with Russian tradition, had not till then played an important role in Soviet expansion. At some point the Soviets realized: mastery of the sea is an essential part of world hegemony! The countries beyond the Eurasian continental bloc can be reached militarily only by sea. In the long run, they cannot be ruled politically without the help of sea power. In this chain of cause and effect lies the motive, and more, even the compelling force behind the U.S.S.R.'s turn to the sea. World revolution is the motor propelling Moscow's naval strategic offensive.

All elements of the Soviet policy of expansion—economic and military "development aid," creation of power positions in the countries of the Third World, naval construction, the offensive naval strategy as well as maritime strategy—are under the same unifying motto. They all have *oceanic sea power* as their final goal. Only with the help of sea power can the continental limits be surmounted, only with sea power can Soviet Russian hegemony be extended over the whole world.

The "peaceful" political-military offensive

In this overall context something else should be mentioned: the atomic balance forces the Soviets to modify their military-political strategy. As long as the U.S.S.R. is unable to render the atomic balance meaningless with massive superiority of force, it cannot use war against the West as a tool of expansion. Expansion must rather be pursued by "peaceful" means without the use of weapons. Military armament is no longer to serve politics as a "continuation with other means," i.e., war—that remains only the *ultima ratio*—but is to serve instead as a tool of peacetime politics. This is not of itself something new. From time immemorial military might has been used as a means of bringing to bear political pressure. It is new that armament should become the direct instrument of politics in peacetime. Power relationships are to be methodically altered with military resources while peace is preserved. The greatest possible military superiority and well-planned demonstration of military might for psychological effect serve this purpose. From the standpoint of demonstrative visibility, the Soviet naval forces are especially well suited to this kind of politics.

This way of using military power for the politics of expansion will be successful only if the military instrument is truly geared to the contingency of war, without prejudice to its "peaceful" employment. Its political effectiveness in peacetime depends on its military value in war. That means that all military considerations, including such as we have presented here, are primarily theoretical models, but certainly not models for playful exercises of the "let's pretend" type. They must be so real that they can at any time withstand a trial by fire.

To that extent the philosophy behind the "peaceful" Soviet strategy resembles the deterrent strategy of NATO: one arms for greatest possible effectiveness in war in order to avoid war. The fundamental difference lies in the ultimate goals: the "peaceful" philosophy of the Soviets is active, is dynamic. It aims at expansion. NATO's is passive, static in nature. It fulfills its mission if a military attack is prevented. Thus the East can widen its sphere of influence, bypassing NATO in the process. The West loses political ground, however. The effects are felt not only in distant regions of the world, but indirectly and directly in our very area. NATO's ability to defend itself is thereby diminished. In the end this may lead to the erosion of NATO, and that is exactly the rationale behind the "peaceful" political-military strategy of the U.S.S.R. When the erosion has proceeded far enough, and when at the same time the atomic balance has been destroyed by massive Soviet superiority, then the military instrument could finally be employed in the sense of hot war. However, if there were no corresponding forces at that time to oppose an aggression from the East, effective use might even be superfluous. The threat would then be so real that all political demands could be realized without difficulty. The Soviets would thus pluck the fruits of their "peaceful" strategy, which they indeed like to call a "strategy of peace" in their propaganda. The end would then be Soviet hegemony and the bolshevization of all Europe and beyond.

Result of the investigation

Against this background of European and global events, we must now draw conclusions from our investigation. Its object is the naval strategic offensive of the Soviets. If the long-term goal of Soviet naval strategy is oceanic sea power, the closing evaluation must focus on this goal. Our questions then are: How well has the Soviets' naval strategic offensive up to now served this goal? How much closer to this goal has it brought them?

Stalin's two big attempts to build a fleet were the product of a continental way of thinking. His strategy did not point beyond coastal defense, even though it included a large submarine fleet for raider warfare on the oceans. Coastal defense and raider warfare are the characteristics of a defensive strategy. Oceanic sea power cannot be established with such a strategy, hegemony cannot be expanded beyond the narrow confines of the European continent.

Nor in the "three waves concept" was an oceanic objective recognizable in the beginning. Its original goal was defensive. But with this concept the Soviets managed, nevertheless, to break off broad zones from Western mastery of the sea, previously all-encompassing and reaching right up to the Soviet coasts. What was not possible with the continental strategy, after the founding of NATO, was to be accomplished by a flanking action from the sea. Soviet strategy in the peripheral seas turned into a naval strategic offensive, at first limited in space. The stronger Soviet naval forces grow, the more difficult becomes the defense of affected NATO nations, Norway, Denmark, and Turkey. Here, it is not just a matter of a peacetime presence that is irrelevant in case of war; here, it is real sea power, based on positions from which Soviet mastery of the sea reaches to the very coastlines of those nations.

Here, Soviet "peace" strategy becomes clearly evident: the threatened countries are to believe the implied suggestion that NATO can no longer defend them. This should lead to their departure from the alliance, to neutralization, and finally to "friendship agreements" with the Soviet Union patterned on Finland's example. A country "befriended" in this manner ultimately falls under Soviet dominion. The same goes for Sweden, now a beneficiary and silent participant in NATO. If this happened as intended, strategy in the peripheral seas would have accomplished its first mission in the framework of the general Soviet strategy of expansion.

The real, the naval strategic, objective goes hand in hand with these limited goals. The inclusion into the Soviet sphere of power of countries situated on the flank of Europe is designed to balance the unfavorable geography of the U.S.S.R. The coasts of those countries are to become the naval strategic positions of the

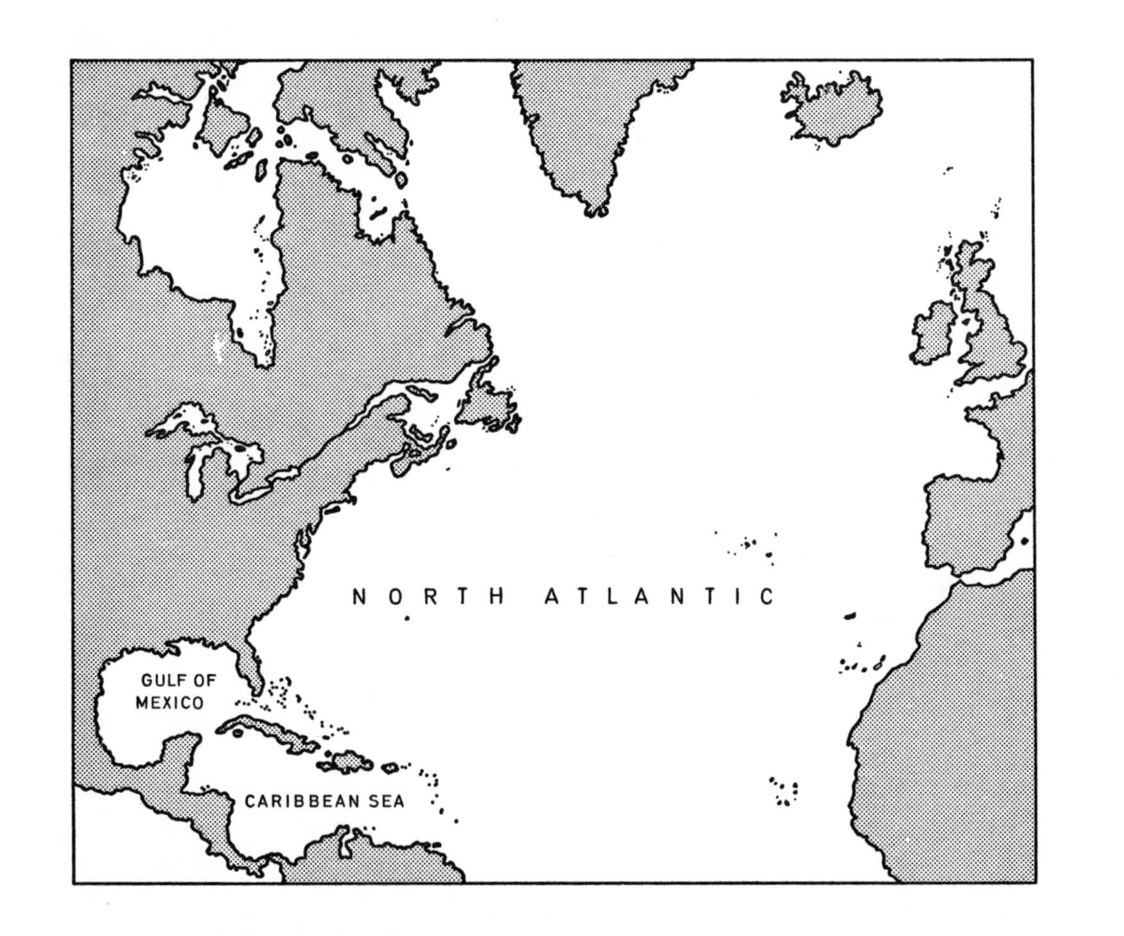
NORTH ATLANTIC
GULF OF MEXICO
CARIBBEAN SEA

Soviet Union in case of war. We have examined the consequences of such an occurrence: the North Sea would come under Soviet mastery, the Black Sea Fleet would become the Soviet Mediterranean Fleet.

However, as bad as that would be for Western defense of Europe by land, the North Sea and the Mediterranean are not part of the oceans. This advance of the Soviet positions still would not put them on the ocean. Nevertheless—and we have discussed this possibility also—once in the Mediterranean, the Soviets would at least have made progress in the direction of one of the three great oceans, the Indian. To complete that purpose they would have to drive the West out of the eastern Mediterranean and replace Western mastery of the sea with their own. The maritime strategy of the Soviets in the eastern Mediterranean and in the northern part of the Indian Ocean rests on the hope that they can succeed in doing just that. From our investigation we know what the devastating consequences of that success would be for the West: the Middle East with its oil, which is so vital to Europe, the entire area round the Persian Gulf, and the adjacent African nations would become part of the Soviet sphere of influence. Therefore, Western mastery of the eastern Mediterranean and Indian Ocean is the only thing that could bring this part of the world to a willing cooperation with the Western nations.

The situation is basically different on the two other large oceans, the Atlantic and the Pacific. On neither can the Soviets obtain genuine naval strategic position in the full definition of the concept. There, maritime strategy fails as a precursor for the establishment of sea power. As long as the mere shadow of Western mastery of the sea existed on these two oceans, no riparian nation—no matter how closely allied with the Soviet Union—would dare place its ports at the disposal of Soviet naval forces in case of war. The decisive element is that no matter where on these two oceans Soviet positions might be located, there would be no secure sea between them and the Eastern bloc. Considering the disadvantage of the Soviet position behind the narrows and the advantage of Western positions on the oceans, all theoretical models of how the Soviets might overcome this handicap operationally or with new weapons—and we have examined them one after another—yield negative results. The "strategy of peace" alone cannot provide them with oceanic sea power on the Atlantic Ocean or the Pacific Ocean.

So long as they do not have naval strategic positions on these oceans, they will be able to conduct warfare against the Western naval forces there only with means that can be employed from their recessed position. That means with submarines and, perhaps in the future, with long-range supersonic aircraft. As we saw, with large numbers of nuclear submarines, the Soviets might possibly bring Western shipping to the point where it broke down. With fast nuclear submarines, they might even eliminate part of the American carrier fleet.

Under extreme circumstances, they could thus make Western mastery of the sea an "empty shell"; they are not yet in a position to do that. Even if they did so, they would not win mastery of the sea for themselves. A situation could conceivably develop in which neither side possessed ocean mastery of the sea and in which a fight for such mastery would not take place. That situation, should it arise, would be a catastrophe for the West, but not for the East. One advantage would remain for the West: its favorable naval strategic positions. With their help and a corresponding armament effort, the West might re-create its sea power.

The anomalous situation in which neither side had mastery of the sea is conceivable only under the condition that both sides possessed a weapon against which there was no effective counterweapon and with which each could destroy the fleet of the other and cause its shipping to break down. We have seen that the fast nuclear submarine could constitute such a weapon. But the West is not completely defenseless against it. As we have pointed out, apart from nuclear depth charges as a last resort, fast hunter/killer submarines, nuclear escort submarines, AS helicopters and helicopter carriers, as well as destroyers specially built for ASW, are available answers. These means should, however, exist in larger numbers than they do now or than is planned. It may well be that all those means would not be effective enough. But sooner or later there will be an effective countermeasure. In the history of naval armament, as in the history of armament in general, there has often been an "ultimate weapon" against which man believed that he would be forever defenseless. But, at last, human ingenuity has always managed to find a counterweapon. Even against intercontinental ballistic missiles, long considered the "ultimate weapon," an answer was found within a decade. The very fast nuclear submarine will not remain the "ultimate weapon" either.

This summary shows the tremendous change in the world-wide naval situation which the Soviets have effected by their naval armament, their offensive naval strategy, and their maritime strategy. And all that without advancing their position and without a foreign policy crisis. The point in time at which we close our investigation is not a pause in the process.

The two naval strategic concepts

Our analysis must not be allowed to end with this summary. The topic would not be exhausted. An evaluating look at the development of the naval strategic concepts of the two great rivals appears in order. Their conceptual evolution is a determining factor for the present state of armament, and hence for the present naval strategic situation.

In the Pacific War, the Americans solved the primary task of their fleet—elimination of the enemy's sea power—by gradually advancing their position. To do this, amphibious operations under fire were necessary, and these operations had to be covered by American carriers. The American Navy had carried the memory of this cooperation between aircraft carriers and amphibious forces into the postwar period. For some time it has been unlikely that a war situation like the one then prevailing would repeat itself. In an East-West war, where would armed action of such dimensions be a real possibility? Where would there be the large army forces required for such big amphibious landings? Obviously, armed action this side of the threshold of full-scale war, that is, in limited war, can still be imagined. Missions of that kind resulted from the American policy of containment in the postwar period. Present American foreign policy, namely withdrawal from its over-engagement overseas, and the general climate of world politics today make it increasingly less likely that the American fleet will in the future be given major amphibious assignments.

Nevertheless, the amphibious concept has played a considerable role for the U.S. Navy in the postwar period. Without properly differentiating between the various situations that might arise, a strong amphibious component was considered indispensable for both peacetime and wartime use. By the same token, the carriers' existence was in large part justified because they had an auxiliary role in amphibious operations in a limited war. The principal mission of maintaining mastery of the oceans was, by comparison, frequently underrated. This tendency was nourished by the fact that the all-encompassing Western mastery of the sea was never seriously threatened in the first two postwar decades. There was so little sign of any threat that in the United States there was earnest debate as to whether a strong carrier fleet was at all necessary to maintain mastery of the sea. It was in fact to the strategic atomic mission, and not to a naval strategic mission proper, that the carrier construction program of the 1950s owed its origin.

Within the U.S. Navy, the carrier concept was clung to as the indispensable guarantor of sea power. To the Navy, the carrier remained the foundation of American naval strategy. But for years it encountered difficulties in convincing public opinion and Congress of the need to build carriers, particularly after the strategic atomic mission shifted from the carriers to the Polaris submarines.

What the U.S. Navy recognized less clearly, and certainly not early enough, was that conditions for aircraft carriers in such non-ocean areas as the Mediterranean and the Norwegian Sea had changed. In these relatively narrow sea areas the carrier had become threatened. As our discussion of the situation in the Norwegian Sea and the Mediterranean has shown, the present author feels that the Americans have not yet taken this change of conditions sufficiently into account.

In this connection one might also believe that in the United States the tasks of naval forces in war have not always been distinguished clearly enough from the arguments in favor of employing a fleet in peacetime. This has created a number of difficulties with the U.S. Congress, which recommended a policy of disengagement overseas before the U.S. government had adopted similar views.

One may say in conclusion that the picture which U.S. naval strategy has presented in the last two decades has not been entirely consistent. Wartime and peacetime tasks, strategic atomic missions, ASW, and amphibious duties—the priorities given each of these have changed several times within this period. It is Moscow's naval strategic offensive and its naval armament that have swept all these priorities off the table. In response there can now be only one, single, uniform naval strategy for the West. It exists now. It is crystal clear and unambiguous. Its objective is to defend mastery of the sea, both on the oceans and in the peripheral seas that are vital to the West, against the Soviet challenge. This wartime mission has first priority. Peacetime use of naval forces, as important as it may be in a given situation, must be subordinated to the requirements of war.

Although the task is clearly recognized today, the developments described above are certainly responsible for the fact that the Soviet challenge hit the U.S. Navy at its "point of greatest weakness," as Admiral Zumwalt testified before the Senate Armed Services Committee.

On the Soviet side also, not everything that glitters is gold. Despite consistency in the building of their fleet, there have been faulty developments and useless investments. On their side, too, the reason is that they have only gradually arrived at a naval strategy of long-term validity. Previously, assignments of the Soviet Navy were the result of momentary evaluations of a given situation. In the beginning, there was coastal defense, that is, the anti-invasion concept and close tactical cooperation with the army; in the next stage there was the strategic atomic threat, which led to the anti-carrier concept. This in turn brought about the broad concept of naval defense, which had the effect of giving them a limited kind of mastery of the sea. The appearance of the Polaris submarines then evoked the antisubmarine concept. Only after the defense against the seaborne nuclear threat had failed twice was the oceanic objective adopted. The changes came in rather quick succession so that the presently existing Soviet fleets still reflect these various steps in development. These fleets are useful instruments for combat in the peripheral seas, but are not for the time being suited for the struggle to gain oceanic mastery of the sea, even setting aside the lack of a naval strategic position.

We may state in conclusion: on both sides, the overall conceptions have matured only fairly recently. The rivalry for mastery of the oceans has only just started. In the process, the Soviet Union is likely to arm itself more quickly than the West. This is particularly disturbing for the West, and could put it in a very delicate position. Yet, in spite of the considerable Soviet armament effort, it should again be stressed that the West holds an invaluable trump card in its more favorable geographic position. Provided it manages to maintain its lead in the field of armament—perhaps in the near future not in terms of numbers, but of quality—it should also manage to maintain oceanic mastery of the sea. One must therefore hope that the American people will concentrate their efforts upon repulsing Moscow's naval strategic offensive. This will require some rethinking and will certainly involve considerable expenditure. The threat which the naval strategic challenge of the Soviets poses for the entire Western world must be clearly recognized in its frightful dimensions. Only then will the need for a defense effort be understood. There is no avoiding the effort if the future of the West is to be safe and detente is to be preserved.

A sea-oriented mentality

We must add one last, overriding item to our final balance, the question of "sea-oriented mentality." Has Soviet Russia, until now a country whose thoughts and actions, judged by historical standards, have been predominantly continental really made itself a genuine sea power?

When Mahan listed the "character of a nation" and the "character of a government" among the elements of sea power, he was thinking of the great sea powers of history, the Phoenicians, the Venetians, the Dutch, and the English. These were nations anchored in the sea by their existence, their prosperity, and their power. People and government knew from long experience what was at stake in the naval wars they conducted. Defeat at sea meant decline, loss of power, or even extinction. When they had to protect their own mastery of the sea or attack that of the enemy, long experience showed them the way.

All these things were lacking in the Soviets' turn to the sea. Endowed as it is with autarky, Russia could live without the sea and without sea power. In a war with a sea power, the U.S.S.R. could be content to defend its own territory. If damage could be done to the enemy at sea, so much the better. Existence would not hinge on it.

The Czars, Lenin, and Stalin thought along such lines. The question to be asked is what brought about the "turn" after Stalin's death? We stand before a mystery. The Soviet Union had already encouraged oceanographic research, had built a deep-sea fishing fleet, and had trained young people in great numbers in such maritime disciplines as naval architecture, naval engineering, and the like. Harbors had been built in the Soviet Union and in underdeveloped countries. All this helped the Soviet Union in its turn to the sea, in its fleet construction, and in its maritime strategy. But were these actions taken in preparation of a later naval strategic offensive, in the framework of long-term premeditation? They can be explained equally well by economic interests and as aids to development.

However one evaluates them, the events after Stalin's death offer anything but a picture of a rationally considered systematic shift from a purely continental to a sea-oriented approach. The new Soviet Navy was born under the auspices of a two-year process of hesitation, of resistance from the marshals of the army, of an order to stop current construction and scrap all the larger ships of the Navy. How is that consistent with the deliberate inception of a new naval strategic era?

Khrushchev, the most powerful man at that time in the Soviet Union, was, at least at first, an outspoken opponent of any naval armament. And yet it was under his aegis that the first missile ships were built, the shipyards were enlarged, and Soviet presence in the Mediterranean began. Again, since Khrushchev, not one of the prominent political personalities in the U.S.S.R. has billed himself as a promoter of the Navy or as an advocate of the naval strategic offensive.

And yet everything that has formed the subject of our analysis was accomplished in this period. Without a doubt, Admiral Gorshkov—and with him the entire Soviet naval officers corps—has played an important role in this development. But how much margin of decision does an individual military personality have in a state like the U.S.S.R.? When one considers the likelihood that the all-powerful Communist Party was previously bound chiefly to the continental tradition, is it thinkable that an admiral overruled the entire Party apparatus and had his own ideas adopted? Other interests were certainly also opposed to fleet construction. After all, money was involved, too.

To a Western observer, these contradictions are incomprehensible. It is, however, a fact that the high command of the Soviet Navy and the unknown forces that have helped to bring the new Soviet fleet into being are now over the hump. Nothing succeeds like success! Now that the Navy has demonstrated convincingly what can be achieved with maritime presence in the name of the strategy of "peace," it is beyond doubt that the naval strategic offensive of the U.S.S.R. is here to stay. The motor of world revolution will push naval development vigorously forward.

In a period of fair weather such as this one, sea-oriented thinking in the U.S.S.R. probably will not have to stand trial. But the time could come when the Soviet Union will be forced, perhaps by increase in China's strength, to concentrate more on continental tasks. It could be that stronger resistance by the West, new technological developments, and, last but not least, the disproportionate geographical positions of East and West would bring to a halt the rapid developments in the direction of oceanic sea power. If that happened, would the sea-oriented mentality still hold the upper hand over the traditional continental approach?

Although it is very difficult to come up with a conclusive answer, the following can be said: In a dictatorship, as elsewhere, a shift from a continental to a sea-oriented way of thinking is conceivable in the minds of only a small circle of people. These people can change. One may assume that the Navy and the naval officers corps will hold high the banner of naval thought for a long time to come. But no one can say how great their influence will be in a dictatorship and against a party in which many people participate in decision-making. The Soviet Navy is not founded upon vital necessity. The driving force is the will for world revolution alone. If this idea were to lose its force, if the dynamics of world hegemony should weaken, then perhaps the Soviet leadership might lapse back into the innate continental Russian way of thinking. But that is indeed a highly speculative thought.

In today's reality, we are facing Soviet imperialism, which is more clearly recognizable than ever before. The West possesses the material means to meet this threat, especially at sea. The fate of the West, in long-term perspective, lies in the mental attitudes of its people. If the West should be defeated, it will not be because of particular weapons systems and strategies. In the end, the decisive factor is the will to hold one's own ground and to defend freedom as the highest good.

index